£1.00

R. LAPTHORN AND COMPANY LIMITED

K.S. GARRETT

Ships in Focus Publications

Published in the UK in 2001 by Ships in Focus Publications,
18 Franklands, Longton
Preston PR4 5PD

Copyright © 2001 K.S. Garrett and Ships in Focus Publications

All rights reserved. No part of this publication may be reproduced, stored in a retrieval system or transmitted in any form or by any means, electronic, mechanical, photocopying, recording or otherwise, without the prior written permission of the copyright owners.

The right of K.S. Garrett to be identified as the author of this work has been asserted by them in accordance with the Copyright, Design and Patent Act 1998.

Printed by Amadeus Press Ltd., Cleckheaton, West Yorkshire
ISBN 1 901 703 41 X

Cover: *Anna Meryl*. *[Fotoflite]*
Back cover top: Sunset from *Hoo Maple*. *[C. Reynolds]*
bottom: *Hoofort*. *[Fotoflite]*

CONTENTS

Tony Lapthorn	Frontispiece
Contents	3
Foreword	5
Introduction	5
Anna Meryl	6
R. Lapthorn and Company Limited	7
Acknowledgements	35
Fleet list	36
Funnel marks	80
Fleet programme	81
Index of ships	87

Tony Lapthorn reunited with the *Nellie*. *[Company archives]*

FOREWORD

Fifty years of operation is a significant milestone in the life of any company. The scale of our achievement has only dawned on me during the past few months when I have had the opportunity of discussing our history with someone outside the company.

I know that the author, Ken Garrett, first met my father more than thirty years ago when he visited him in what father still describes as 'the wooden bathing hut on the seawall in the big city of Hoo'. He had more contact with us in later years when a number of coastal shipping companies joined together to form the Small Ships Training Group. Here, in addition to training, we discussed many other matters of mutual interest. With his thirty years' experience of the Lapthorn family, it came as some surprise when Ken expressed his wish to write this book.

Quite rightly, the contents of many of these pages are concerned with the individual lives of the vessels that have passed through our hands, however fleetingly. But, any company will have employed personalities, whatever its business. In our case, there were the bargemen of the 1950s, many of whom moved on to the coasters of the intermediate years. They have been followed by the international crews of today. It is true to say that the most difficult part of running ships has been, and probably always will be, finding the right seafarers to do the job and then to retain them. Consequently, we are very grateful to the many individuals who have served with us, especially those who have spent over twenty years with the company, both afloat and ashore.

As he has trawled through various written records and the archives of the minds of the principal players, Ken has unearthed craft and events that have rekindled memories and ignited some lively family discussions. Strangely, the speed of change in the last few years has made recent events more difficult to recall in detail. However, it may simply be that the early years were much more exciting.

I am certain of one thing. Those who follow will have, through this book, access to many of the events, people and craft that have been the past and form the basis for the future. To them I say 'Keep your records. You will have enormous fun preparing the centenary edition.'

DAVID LAPTHORN
Hoo
January 2001

INTRODUCTION

It has been a great pleasure to write this book to coincide with the celebrations to mark both the company's fiftieth anniversary and the eightieth birthday of the founder Tony Lapthorn. These are no mean achievements when viewed against the contemporary background. Many enterprises had their beginnings in the immediate post war years but few, particularly in shipping, have shown the same tenacity nor survived successfully for fifty years and, under succeeding generations, continue to give every indication of carrying on for another fifty years. In the early days it was very much hand to mouth and at times, decidedly touch and go, but hard work, dedication and a loyal team pulled the company through.

I first met Tony in 1968 and although working for one of his competitors for many years I have always admired him and his company and hold them in the highest regard. I would like to take the opportunity of offering my congratulations and best wishes for the future to Tony and Rachel, to their sons David and John and their families, and to all those who have worked for the company over the years.

Many people have been involved with the company, some for many years, ashore and afloat. Some, but by no means all, are mentioned in the narrative and I offer my apologies to those whose efforts have gone unrecorded.

I would like to thank all those who helped in the preparation of this book and in particular, Tony and David Lapthorn who willingly gave me their time and cheerfully submitted to my questioning. While every effort has been made to ensure accuracy and a balanced view, any errors contained herein and the opinions expressed are mine alone.

KEN GARRETT
East Malling
January 2001

Anna Meryl. [Fotoflite incorporating Skyfotos]

R. LAPTHORN AND COMPANY LIMITED

J.A. Lapthorn, early days
John Anthony Lapthorn (Tony) was born at Radlett in Hertfordshire in June 1921. His father, Arnold Roy Lapthorn (Roy), was a chartered accountant and in 1927 the family moved to Lee-on-the-Solent when Roy became a partner in Edmonds, Clover and Ackery of Portsmouth. Roy's father Edwin, a director of Ratsey and Lapthorn Ltd., the sailmakers of Gosport, Cowes, Gourock and New York, had decided that the days of sail were over and insisted that his son took up accountancy and did not follow him into the family business. From a trading ship point of view this might have been an accurate forecast but it overlooked the vast and growing area of sails used in the leisure industry. Despite this setback, Roy had picked up an interest in sailing from his father's business and this was, in turn, passed on to his son Tony.

Tony went to Edinburgh House preparatory school at Lee-on-the-Solent and then to Oundle from 1933 to 1940. He left school to become an apprentice naval architect with J.I. Thornycroft and Co. Ltd. of Woolston. Unfortunately, his father died, aged only 51, in 1941 and towards the end of the year Tony, despite being in a reserved occupation, joined the Royal Air Force and was posted to the Marine Section. Attempts were made to dissuade him, even to the day when he went to Portsmouth station to get the train to Cardington for his basic training. The Rail Transport Officer turned him back because he did not have the correct release documents from his employer but he was determined and managed to obtain the documents on the same day.

After initial training he was posted to India for three and a half years and became a leading aircraftsman. He was based at the Karachi flying boat base at Karangi Creek from where the PBY-5 Catalinas patrolled the Persian Gulf. Originally he lived in tented accommodation, later huts but, finally, reasonably comfortable buildings were provided. He was asked to produce some dinghies to carry flarepath lights to assist flying boat operations at night. Tony designed the dinghies and using a large, aircraft packing case as a workshop he built the craft using timber taken from other packing cases. The craft had masts with lights atop and were moored in line along one side of the flarepath and the lights would be switched on to assist the flying boats. They were successful and as a result, South East Asia Command ordered ninety similar dinghies from a boat builder in Karachi. Tony supervised the building of these very superior craft of double-skin teak hulls with copper fastenings. After the war, Tony received an Award to Inventors of £25 for his work.

Later, Tony went to Calcutta and worked with the DGSR (Director General, Shipbuilding and Repair) and became involved with Commander Lloyd Roberts. In pre-war days he was a Lloyd's surveyor and had been commissioned into the Royal Corps of Naval Constructors. Returning to Lloyds Register after the war, Commander Roberts became Senior Surveyor in the Medway area. Some large cargo barges were converted into mobile air-sea rescue bases for the Burma campaign and a sampan was converted into a 'zero decibel' motor spy craft for operations on the Irrawaddy river. Tony also spent some time supervising repairs to landing craft to the detriment of his RAF work and was threatened with a disciplinary charge by a visiting Air Force officer but the threat was withdrawn.

Demobilisation
With the war over, Tony returned home, was demobbed in 1946 and went to work with the boat builders C.A. Purbrook Ltd. at Christchurch. His father, Roy Lapthorn, had built a small sailing boat on the continent during the First World War using whatever timber came to hand and managed to get it to England after the war. It was called *Coot* and he gave the design to Charles Purbrook who built many of them. The Anglo-Iranian Oil Company Sailing Club at Abadan in the Persian Gulf purchased a number and the order was repeated after the Second World War.

Tony had some differences of opinion with Charles Purbrook, left and turned his hand to fishing. At first he sailed with his friend Bob Bishop but later he bought his own boat. She was a converted ship's lifeboat called *Richmea* and had a two-cylinder Brit petrol/paraffin engine. It was hard work but a good living could be had, particularly with sole fished from the Christchurch Ledge. The main problem was to find regular crew; most did not want to return to sea whilst they still had money in their pocket, leaving him short-handed.

However, it was not all work in this busy post-war period and in 1947 Tony married Rachel Dibley in Lee-on-the-Solent. He bought the Z 4-ton class *Sara*, designed by Dr. Harrison Butler of metacentric shelf fame, intending to live aboard but soon bought the sailing barge *Leslie* (43/1894) to use instead. John Scott Hughes, the yachting correspondent of the *Times* newspaper, had recently sold the barge to John Briant, who later sold it to Tony for conversion. He converted the barge into a houseboat at the yard of John Briant's Whitewall Barge, Yacht and Boat Co. Ltd., in Whitewall Creek at Frindsbury and sailed it back to Christchurch. The barge *Leslie* was the family home and was never part of the trading fleet but nevertheless is included in the fleet list.

Whitewall experience
John Briant was very impressed by Tony's expertise in converting the *Leslie* and offered him a manager's job at the yard that he accepted in 1948. Sailing back with the *Leslie* he was caught out by a gale off Dover and had to be towed in by J. Walker, a local boatman. It transpired that one of the lee boards had come adrift making the barge all but unmanageable. He sailed next day. During the trip, on 17th October 1948, his son David was born in Bournemouth. With his crew he travelled back, by train, to see his son and celebrate.

The Whitewall Barge, Yacht and Boat Company had found Whitewall Creek too congested for their expansion plans and bought some land at Hoo, previously brickfields, from Walter C.W. Brice of Walter St. John Brice. The move took place during 1949 and 1950. John Briant had ambitious plans to expand into boat building, repairing and conversions, slipways and a marina but unfortunately did not have the necessary resources and the company went bankrupt in 1951. Tony also lost because he had made some personal guarantees and found himself in debt. With loans from his family he paid off the debts but vowed never to get himself into such a predicament again.

Hoo St. Werburgh
Despite all the attendant problems, the family settled at Hoo St. Werburgh, a village on the banks of the Medway. In

existence since Roman times, the name means high or hill in Anglo-Saxon. It is a relative term to describe the place that certainly rises above the adjacent estuary saltings. St. Werburgh was a devout Saxon princess born between AD 640 and 650 and a member of the Mercian royal household. Her uncle, King Ethelrede, gave her charge of all the religious houses under Mercian influence including a convent at Hoo. She became the subject of the Miracle of Hoo when, being molested and chased by an evil man, she was swept up into an oak tree and safety. She died in AD 698 or 699 and, although her original burial site is unknown, it is assumed to have been within the Kingdom of Mercia in the south east of England. Her elevation to sainthood took place in AD 708 and, because of the threat of Danish invasion, her remains were taken to safer ground at Chester in AD 875. A stone shrine dedicated to her memory was erected in 1310 and still stands in the cathedral.

The Lapthorn family's move to Hoo was to prove unexpectedly beneficial once the Whitewall problems had been overcome. Several opportunities presented themselves, enabling Tony to get a fresh start in a way that still has echoes fifty years later.

Bricks, tiles and earthenware pots had been made at Hoo since earliest times and shipped out by barge through Hoo Creek from Buttercrock Wharf. Most of this manufacturing had finished by the late 1930s and much of the land has now been reclaimed and used for housing developments. The site of the Hoo Brick Company is now the Hoo Marina Homes Park. Solomon J. Brice, who had been involved in the local extraction of mud for bricks and cement, also the rough goods trade from London, could see the end of this traditional work and diversified into agriculture and the trade in sand and gravel, also known as aggregates or ballast. It was this last, taken up by his son Walter Brice, that was to have such a profound effect on the Lapthorn business. Brice had obtained a contract to supply sand and gravel for the building of the Kent Oil Refinery on the Isle of Grain and Tony could see the aggregates being brought to Hoo by motor barges and taken on to the construction site by lorries.

Early operations
In August 1951 the barge *Nellie* of 110 deadweight tons was purchased for £150. The gear was taken out and she was converted into a motor barge with a government-surplus Chrysler Crown engine for about £1,000. During the conversion, Tony paid the Receiver for the use of the Whitewall berth and facilities. The business got under way when Tony asked Walter Brice to let him carry aggregates from Gibb's Wharf at Grays to Brice's Wharf at Hoo. Brice agreed and a rate of 6/- per cubic yard was set. The ballast trade became the core business and was developed, using converted motor barges and later by motorships.

Wages were paid according to the share system. For example, the *Nellie* carried 90 cubic yards and at 6/- per yard the freight paid for each trip was £27. Payment was not instantaneous and Tony had to go to the Brice office to ask for the cheque. As owner, he took half of this; the master would receive two thirds and the mate one third of the other half. To encourage frugality the crew paid for the fuel and food out of their share. Even when sailing as master himself, money was tight and margins small. On the first trading day, 27th November 1951, a Shell lorry driver delivering tractor vaporising oil (TVO) to the *Nellie* demanded £5 in advance before he would make delivery.

The *Leslie* was sold in 1951 and the growing family moved into the larger *Alice May*. A small office was made in the fore end of the barge from where the company was run. Accounts were kept by Tony's wife Rachel and crews would come here to be paid their share of the freight earnings, usually on a weekly basis. The more provident amongst them banked their money in Hoo village without delay. Originally, the *Alice May* was berthed at Hoo Marina but was later moved to the nearby Buttercrock Wharf.

From November 1951 the barges were registered in Rachel's name, by which means it was hoped to keep any latent creditors away from the barges, and the company became known as R. Lapthorn and Company. Tony's grandfather, Edwin Lapthorn, had formed an affection for Belgium and the Belgian people. He took their national colours of black, red and yellow when he designed a 'bob' for his sailing craft and developed the present design which Tony adopted for his own houseflag. The same design was used for the funnel mark when he started to own ships. Edwin Lapthorn is understood to have believed in the Belgian 'cause' which probably refers to the international outrage at the invasion and subsequent harsh treatment of neutral Belgium by the German execution of their Schlieffen plan in 1914.

Nellie inward bound to Hoo Creek. *[Company archives]*

Early incidents
The *Nellie* provided Tony with some excitement on 17th December 1952 when entering the Medway loaded with sand. There was a north westerly gale and when he rounded Grain Spit, with the weather on his starboard quarter, he was pooped and the engine room skylight carried away. The engine room was partially flooded and the engine stopped. Tony and his mate, Bill Hopewell-Smith, managed to pump it out, restarted the engine and also set a small sail making it possible to proceed to leeward. Later, the engine stopped again and they managed to put the barge ashore and dropped the anchor off Minster. Some blankets soaked in TVO were set alight in the rigging and the Southend lifeboat soon arrived and landed them at Southend. They were given some new clothes by the Shipwrecked Fishermen and Mariners' Royal Benevolent Society and put into bed and breakfast accommodation for the night before being returned to Hoo. Tony recalls that this was the one and only time in his life that he had to share

a bed with another man! The following day, Tony took the *Sally* loaded up with pumps, shovels and men down to the barge. She had drifted during the night and somehow ended up on the eastern side of the remains of the wartime boom defence with her anchor on the western side. She was pumped out and happily, floated at the next high water and towed back to Hoo. Her wheelhouse and hatchcovers were gone but otherwise she appeared in good condition. As a bonus, the company was even paid for salvaging the cargo.

The barge was out of action for about a month during which time the disastrous east coast flooding had taken place. Her first job when returning to work was a month's time charter assisting with repairs to the sea wall around the Kent Oil Refinery which had been inundated just before it was due to be commissioned. The rate was £12 per day plus food from the US contractors who had a special dispensation from the Ministry of Food. Barge food was generally pretty basic but it improved marvellously with the addition of such American delicacies as tinned ham and peaches. The bags of clay for repairing the walls were tipped down a chute into the barge from a lorry and on one occasion the bags stuck on the lorry tail and it looked as though the lorry itself was about to embark. The driver made a swift evacuation from his cab but after pivoting dangerously for a minute or so, the bags slipped and the lorry remained ashore.

Even after the immediate repairs to the coastal defences, the aftermath of the east coast floods brought more work. More sand and gravel was required to build up the retaining sea walls of the new refinery providing work for another two years. It's an ill wind!

More acquisitions
Meanwhile, other barges were purchased with Mrs Rachel Lapthorn as the registered owner. The *Lancashire*, as a constructive total loss, came from Wakeley Brothers in 1953 followed by the *Mildreda* and *Pride of Sheppey* both purchased from Andrews and Strevens of Sittingbourne in 1954.

The sailing barge *Felix* was purchased in 1955 and kept under sail for about a year with Alec Josh as the skipper. This made her one of the last spritsail barges regularly in trade under sail alone until she was fitted with a Chrysler Crown engine. Once a month she took stores to the

Felix. [T. Farnham collection]

Nellie alongside *Gladys* at Gibbs Wharf, London. *[Company archives]*

Norwegian tanker *Irex* (8,250/1953) while she was discharging Venezuelan crude oil at Berry Wiggins' jetty at Kingsnorth. The *Alice May*, returned to trade as a motor barge after the family moved ashore to High Halstow in 1956, was also involved in the stores run on occasions.

The barge *R.S. Jackson* was purchased from Solomon Brice early in 1953 for use as a store. She was not in good condition and was not intended for trade. Later in the year, her job done, she was offered to the Sea Scouts at Newhaven. Tony's friend, Bob Bishop, towed her with his fishing boat *Ocean Viking* but unfortunately the tow parted off Folkestone and the barge was never seen again, presumed sunk.

The motor barge *Gladys* became what was probably the first craft managed by Lapthorn for another owner. She had been purchased by Don Carmichael in 1954 when the gear was removed and two Kelvin engines fitted. She was engaged in the ballast trade for a couple of years before being sold for conversion to a barge yacht in 1956. With her new owner she made some extensive passages but unfortunately came to grief in 1960 when she hit a Russian ship anchored near the Grain Edge Buoy.

Darling Brothers of London had a contract with Imperial Chemical Industries Ltd. for the transhipment and storage of explosives on the Thames. A coaster, usually the *Lady Anstruther* (547/1946) or sometimes *Saint Bedan* (452/1937), would bring the cargo from the factory at Ardeer on the west coast of Scotland and it would be transhipped into barges at the Chapman Anchorage. The loaded barges would then lie in the Lower Hope until the cargo was required for export. In the evening, an empty barge would take the stevedores back to Gravesend and tie up overnight before taking the men out the next morning.

ICI had some of their own barges, acquired from the Successors to T.F. Wood Ltd. of Gravesend, but Jack Darling bought the *Revival* and *Water Lily* for the trade and these were managed by Lapthorn from 1957. *Alice May*, back in commission and converted for the trade, was later joined by the *Felix*, re-engined with a four cylinder Perkins engine.

Towage 1
Before buying any motor barges for trade, Tony had bought the Faversham-registered fishing boat *Sally* (F 96) and used her for various jobs including towing. At the time he was not too sure which direction his business was going to take and it seemed sensible to maintain the fishing registry. She had a Chrysler Crown engine that was later replaced by a four-cylinder, 56 horsepower Perkins unit. Despite her low power, the *Sally* carried out many estuary and sea tows. At the time, there were many surplus motor launches and motor torpedo boats being towed around to be used as houseboats or to be broken up to get at the copper. They were difficult to manage when towed bow first and, although slower, it was easier to tow them stern first. Eight Esso fuelling pontoons, built by Harland and Wolff Ltd. at North Woolwich, were towed to such places as Ramsgate and as far afield as Brixham. The contract was held by Gaselee and Son Ltd., who towed the pontoons to Queenborough, but it did not fit in with their normal work and the crews of their large tugs were happy that the rest of the tow was subcontracted.

A ship's lifeboat, reputed to have come originally from the *Queen Mary* but converted into a tug, was purchased in 1955. She too was re-engined with a four-cylinder Perkins engine. Tony was looking for a suitable name and in his own words, 'Some twit suggested *Hooray*'. The suggestion was used and thus became the start of the famous line of *Hoo* names. She was quite a superior craft of double-diagonal mahogany construction with teak gunwhale capping. She was double ended, thirty two feet long and when properly ballasted drew five feet aft to submerge the twenty eight inch propeller. Also engaged in towing surplus motor launches she carried out some lengthy tows for such a small craft. She was later sold locally and renamed *Freeboy*.

The former War Department *Crystal II* was acquired in 1961 and renamed *Hooligan*. Her original Widdop engine 'hydraulicked' and was replaced by a six-cylinder 125 horsepower Perkins engine. One evening,

Dick Hazell of Gaselee telephoned Tony and told him that the *Lune Fisher* (1,012/1962) was adrift in an easterly gale and calling for assistance. He drove to Harwich where the *Hooligan* was berthed and mobilised the tug. The casualty was located in moderating weather and Tony made fast with his own nylon towing spring. Using the tides he managed to tow the ship into Felixstowe and safety.

The tugs were also engaged in towing lighters loaded with steel fabrications, piles and other equipment for the Kent Oil Refinery at the Isle of Grain for McAlpines and similar cargoes to the Kingsnorth Power Station for Laings. A launch with a limited towing capacity was purchased in the early 1960s and named *Hoodwink*. She was bought for the work to Kingsnorth Power Station, towing barges loaded with piles and also acted as a safety boat.

From time to time these craft were chartered to carry out other tasks and one in particular involved towing a barge with compressors and other gear to assist in the underwater cleaning of the foul bottom of a tanker discharging at the Isle of Grain. The *Hooligan* became involved in tests of flotation rings for the containment of oil at the Isle of Grain for British Petroleum. The rings were deployed around the 'spill' and the tug attempted to clean up with suction hoses.

Surveying
Sally, fitted with an echo sounder and other navigational devices, was used on a number of surveying contracts. Initially, surveys of Brightlingsea Creek and Martins Farm Pits were carried out for Brimac (Brice and McAlpine). Later, on charter to Kelvin Hughes and equipped with more sophisticated gear, the vessel was used on a number of public works undertakings. Surveys for sewer outfalls were carried out off St. Bees Head and Workington for the Cumbria County Council. Oil companies provided much business with surveys of Baglan Bay, Port Talbot for British Petroleum, Fawley and Spithead for Esso. The Varne Bank was surveyed in connection with a wreck clearance project. Other work included a study of tidal flows at the Isle of Grain.

John Chancellor spent some time on the *Sally* when she was engaged on surveying, was relief master on the later motor ships and was also employed ashore on re-rigging sailing barges and similar work. He became a director of the company but eventually left to concentrate on his artistic interests.

First motor ship
Stan and Chick Yeates, husband and wife, were skipper and mate of the Cunis barge *Glenmore* (61/1902) and they first met Tony at the Hoo Ness Yacht Club. Later, they were lying weatherbound at Queenborough with a cargo of fertilizer for Ipswich when Tony came alongside with the *Nellie*. He had a cargo of salvaged rolls of paper taken from the sea wall after the 1953 floods. Tony went aboard the *Glenmore* and heard that they were proposing to buy the barge *Valdora* (56/1904) from Sully Brothers. He told them that he had a contract to ship ballast for Brice and was looking for a good strong ship and help with the finance. They were interested.

Later, Tony contacted Stan and Chick again and said that he had not yet found a suitable ship but invited them to join him anyway. He offered them the *Felix* but Stan was not interested in taking a purely sailing barge in the ballast trade. As an alternative, Tony offered them the *Nellie* which they accepted. After about six months Tony acquired the *Mary Birch* with their help. She had sunk off Saltend after a collision with the trawler *Loch Moidart* (550/1947); raised and beached she was later towed into Hull. The Yeates and their engineer, Peter Hebdon, joined during the subsequent repairs. They loaded a cargo of fertiliser at Immingham Dock for Ipswich that caused all sorts of bother because the local Board of Trade surveyor insisted upon a freeboard survey. The owners considered this unnecessary since the vessel was destined to trade within estuarial limits once she arrived in the Thames. In the event a temporary certificate was issued for a single voyage requiring a three foot freeboard. This gave her a draft of about 3 foot 6 inches and she could only load 120 tons, about half her anticipated deadweight. Despite this little local difficulty, the Yeates settled down and remained in the *Mary Birch* for about ten years.

Sally. [Company archives]

One evening in late October 1956 after loading in the Colne, the Yeates declined to sail due to very bad weather and tied up for the night. Another 'Beetle', as the X lighters were called, *Alpheus* with skipper Geoff Maynard had also loaded for the Thames and coming alongside, discussed the weather, explaining that he was very much in two minds about sailing. He was keen to get to Plumstead where his baby son was shortly to have an operation. For whatever reason he sailed during the night and was not seen again.

During 1958 Tony was asked to go to Ireland to survey another 'Beetle', *Dingle*, on behalf of John Hobbins, a former skipper with the London and Rochester Trading Co. Ltd. The *Dingle* was in poor condition and Tony advised against it but proposed, instead, the Danish-owned *Peterna*, another member of the class. The ship was purchased and Lapthorns carried out the technical and commercial management.

More ballast work had come with the building of the M2 Motorway. It was taken to Crown Wharf at Sittingbourne or to Cuxton. For some time the Yeates had the *Mary Birch* running turn and turn about with John Hobbins and his wife Jill on their *Peterna*. There was no proper berth at Cuxton and they had to make fast on one of the massive piles. A crane barge discharged the cargo but the bridge site was too far upriver to get in and out on the same tide and always took at least two. Jill and Chick both liked to have fresh milk for their tea and had an arrangement whereby they would each leave a pint at the berth when they sailed for the other to pick up on arrival.

Mary Birch was soon joined by the *Mavis*; built of iron she was originally a ketch but had been converted to a twin screw motor ship. Her former owners, S.W. Tar Distillers Ltd., had placed tanks in her hold and used the ship to carry tar in Shoreham harbour. After purchase, her tar tanks were removed and she reverted to a dry cargo ship. The original two-cylinder Ellwe and two-cylinder Bolinders engines were replaced by a four-cylinder Perkins engine with a single screw on the starboard side. She was reckoned to be a handy little craft and easy to manoeuvre although rather tender. She carried ballast to the Tunnel

Mary Birch. [J. Thompson]

The ship was a former X lighter, one of a numerous class built for the navy in 1915. They were forerunners of modern landing craft and some of them were used in the Dardanelles campaign. The significance to Lapthorn lies in the fact that here we have for the first time a steel motor ship, built as such rather than a cut down and converted wooden sailing barge.

Mary Birch and *Peterna* at Hoo. [S. Yeates]

Mary Birch and *Mavis* at Wandsworth. *[J. Thompson]*

Jetty at Thurrock where a new outer jetty was being constructed. Her 120 tons of cargo was just sufficient to fill one of the tubular concrete piles. During the discharge, *Mavis* had to moor uncomfortably athwart the tide.

The ballast trade
The ballast trade became the core business of the company and paradoxically, despite the relatively low value of the cargo and the basic nature of the early motor barges and ships, it required a sophisticated approach. Loading places were not chosen for ease of access but to be close to the gravel workings; similarly, discharging points needed to be adjacent to the point of use, otherwise transport costs would escalate. Many of these berths were situated up narrow, winding tidal creeks and the skippers needed special knowledge to negotiate them safely with the biggest cargo the circumstances would permit. Use of pilots was anathema and in any event the costs would have made the job uneconomic. An understanding of the tides and the depths of water in the creeks and on the berths was a crucial element in making a successful voyage. Experience was essential in deciding how much cargo to load particularly as the vessel would often be aground when loading was completed and even if afloat it was sometimes difficult to read the draft. All these variables made strict adherence to the loadline rules a trifle academic. Generally speaking, these craft operated within the 'Smooth Water Area' in the Thames Estuary to the west of a line that was drawn between Colne Point in Essex and Whitstable in Kent during winter months and a little further out, between Clacton Pier and Reculvers in the summer. The regulations enabled them to load to a lesser freeboard and thus carry a larger cargo than if they were proceeding to sea. This presented an interesting navigational anomaly because the sandbanks and channels in the estuary run along the tidal line and do not conform to any arbitrary line drawn north to south. To proceed along the Thames or into the Medway from the entrance of the Colne it is first necessary to go just outside the area to cross the Spitway before entering the East Swin channel.

As with many bulk cargoes there were frequently arguments about the out turn weight of cargo; to counter these and to improve the rate of discharge, the *Mary Birch* had her holds boarded from the coamings down and also transverse bulkheads. Lines were drawn at calculated levels on the boarding to indicate the capacity. A custom of the trade, it is interesting to note that ballastmen always talked in yards and not tons. It is therefore not always easy to arrive at the deadweight tonnage. For example, *Mary Birch* loaded about 180 cubic yards; other sources indicate that she had a deadweight of about 220 tons and these two figures are generally compatible. Cargo density depended upon the size of the material and 3/8" shingle stowed at about 1 ton/cubic yard while sand and stone graded from 1.5" to zero stowed about 1.5 tons/cubic yard. An average, rule of thumb figure of 1.25 tons/cubic yard is a rough guide. Nowadays of course, it is normal to talk in terms of cubic metres and metric tonnes.

There were a number of loading points, one of the earliest to be used was Gibbs Wharf at Grays. Later, other sites further along the Essex coast were used including Martins Farm Pits at Brightlingsea, Fingringhoe, Freshwater, Fullbridge, Rowhedge and later still at Felixstowe.

Defining moment
In the early days, Tony Lapthorn adopted a very hands-on approach and sailed his ships himself. He did not have to pay himself a wage and, apart from living expenses and crew wages, the barge's earnings could be put back into the business. By leading from the front and being an example to his crews he was able to keep the momentum going. This was possible when he only had a couple of relatively simple motor barges to concern him but as time passed and he owned a fleet, albeit small, things got more complicated and there were other demands on his time. Walter Brice told him that he could not run his business from the deck of a weather-bound barge off Brightlingsea. Reluctantly he took the advice and came ashore in 1954 to manage affairs, but his crews were encouraged in the certain knowledge that the Guv'nor was always willing and able to do it all himself again.

The opportunity was also taken to consolidate the business affairs and the limited company was formed in

November 1954 becoming R. Lapthorn and Company Limited. The registered office was the sailing barge *Alice May* at Buttercrock Wharf, Hoo. A small office was built on the wharf when the barge went back into service and three or four people ran the business. Despite some local moves the office still bears the same name. The present office, just a little east of the old site, was opened in June 1987. An extension was added in June 1997 and now provides accommodation for 22 staff; a far cry from those early days.

Work for Bowater
The Bowater Paper Corporation Ltd. owned a fleet of wooden lighters and a tug, *Elizabeth Murre* (46/1930), to tow the lighters loaded with china clay from Ridham Dock to the paper mill at Kemsley. The tug would then tow the lighters, loaded with paper, from the mill to the buoys at Queenborough. When the Bowater tug was out of service for repair or survey, Lapthorns were asked to provide a relief. Either *Sally* or *Hooray* was used, depending upon which was available.

As a result of the direct contact, the company was offered a number of the wooden Bowater lighters with their Commonwealth city names. The price was agreed at £30 each; as is, where lies. The rotten *Durban* was thrown in for nothing provided it was towed away. When Tony Lapthorn arrived to take delivery of the first lighters he found that the dockmaster, Captain Jackson, had removed all the tarpaulins and no amount of argument could persuade him that they were part of the deal.

Sometime later, an Admiralty Agent called at the Lapthorn office because, apparently, they now owned the only suitable wooden lighters in the country and one was urgently required for magnetic mine experiments. The *Durban*, now lying on a mud berth at Hoo, was offered for £1,000 and a shipwright was summoned from H.M. Dockyard at Chatham to carry out a survey. He pronounced her rotten and the better *Belmont* was offered for £3,000. She passed survey and was taken away. Two more of them were chartered to the Medway Bridge contractors. They damaged one that was then declared a constructive total loss and the underwriters paid £500.

The *Adelaide*, partially laden with china clay, had a curious problem at Ridham Dock during the 1960s. She had lain empty during some very hot weather while a dockers' strike was taking place and her upper strakes had dried out. When the dockers returned to work, they started to load her with china clay for the mill at Kemsley. The crane was loading the lighter normally from aft, forward but instead of working to a finish as Lapthorn's lighterman Les Rogers had expected, the dockers knocked off at 5 pm leaving the lighter well down by the stern with her bow in the air. The seams had opened in the heat and she leaked badly, taking in so much water that she sank during the night and slipped under the ship she had been lying alongside. Her disappearance naturally caused some consternation but she was soon spotted and a Gaselee tug managed to pull her clear at the next high water. She was dumped unceremoniously on the adjacent marshes and left to rot.

A number of other lighters were purchased, some swim head and others of various shapes from the Chatham Dockyard and elsewhere, most of them were soon sold on. Two of the dockyard lighters with particularly fine lines were very difficult to tow in line and continually took a sheer one way or another. They became more docile and manageable if lashed side by side. When purchased, few of the lighters had names and most were unregistered. They were given some extraordinary but apposite names, *Hoo Doo*, *Dr. Hoo*, *Hoos Hoo*, *Hoo Ha*, *Hooch* and so on.

Stan Yeates frequently towed the lighters from Ridham to Kemsley in the tug *Hooray* with Les Rogers on the quay to help him. Getting out of the dock he used to keep parallel to the berth and head right across the river; usually, the last lighter of the tow would just clear the opposite berth and the tow would stream out in line astern on the tide.

The work for Bowater continued until the early 1970s when the paper manufacturer arranged supplies of china clay using special railway wagons from Cornwall and Devon brought directly into the mill. Not only did the company lose out on the towage and lighterage business but other coastal shipping companies also lost contracts for the shipping of china clay from the south west ports to Ridham Dock and Northfleet.

Sally. [Company archives]

*Hooness at Jersey.
[D. Hocquard]*

The Gaselee connection
During the busy period working for Bowaters, the company formed a close working relationship with Gaselee and Son Ltd. that influenced affairs for years. Gaselee, in the towage business since 1879, had held the contract to tow the lighters for Edward Lloyd and later Bowater, onward to London and return them empty to Queenborough, since 1895. Coincidentally, Gaselee also held the contract for ship towage on the Swale from the Medway to Ridham Dock when it was built by Edward Lloyd in the 1920s.

The relationship with Gaselee was taken a considerable step further on 20th October 1963 when they bought 60% (87 of the issued 145) of the Lapthorn shares. Gaselee, whose operations had been dominated by towage in the Port of London and the enclosed docks, had come to the conclusion that there was little future for them there and wished to diversify their activities. Not wishing to have any minority shareholders, Stan Yeates was bought out and was no longer part owner of the *Mary Birch*.

The capital raised on the sale of shares enabled the company to build a new ship, *Hooness*, at J.W. Cook and Co. Ltd. at Wivenhoe in 1965. A sister vessel, *Edward Stone* was built for the Eddystone Shipping Co. Ltd. and bareboat chartered to Lapthorn. The company later purchased the ship. Named after Mrs. Brice's father, the ship inevitably picked up the nickname of Ted Grit.

In May 1964, Lapthorn and Gaselee joined with the shipper Kersten Hunik, the majority shareholder, to form the East Anglian Shipping Co. Ltd. The purpose was to operate a regular freight service between Lowestoft and Rotterdam. The service was started by the *Yarvic* and the *Edward Stone* was also involved. The venture was not as profitable as had been hoped and in 1968, Lapthorn and Gaselee sold their shares to Kersten Hunik.

Edward Stone. [Company archives]

Alice May in West India Dock, London during later years. *[C.C. Beasley]*

Branching out

From the early 1950s it could be seen that the ballast work for the Kent Oil Refinery, the M2 Motorway and other local public work contracts would tail off and alternative employment would have to be found. One of the earliest additions was the fertiliser trade; sulphate of ammonia and triple superphosphate, usually from the Beckton Gas Works to Faversham and elsewhere. The barge *Lancashire* had capsized in the Crouch and was bought as a constructive total loss, her gear was removed and a Chrysler Crown engine, a wheelhouse and hatch covers were fitted. Just over a year after her purchase she was moored for the night at Beckton Gas Works waiting to load a cargo of sulphate of ammonia. Before turning in for the night the crew had banked up the stove and placed the Tilly lamp on top, presumably to keep it warm for the morning. During the night the wind freshened, drawing the fire and apparently the lamp exploded setting fire to the forecastle accommodation. Luckily the crew were uninjured but had time only to leap out of their bunks, scramble on deck and up the ladder to the jetty above. It was a bitterly cold night and they were pitifully cold by the time the Fire Brigade arrived. The barge was not worth repairing and she was eventually buried in a landfill site at Maldon after being used for a while as a loading pontoon.

Other cargoes presented themselves according to circumstances. For example, during the 1953 floods the Bowater warehouses at Northfleet were flooded, soaking the rolls of paper that swelled and burst the walls. Many floated off into the river and were later left by the receding floodwaters spread over fields on the Essex side. They were now the property of Bowater's underwriters who sold

Mary Birch loading beech boles at St.Valery sur Somme. *[J. Thompson]*

them to a salvage agent who promptly resold them to Bowater. They were collected and taken to Gibbs Wharf at Grays from where they were taken to Kemsley for repulping. Some of the rolls had grass and reeds growing out of them by the time they were shipped and had to be handled very carefully.

Another source of business stemming from the floods was the movement of crates of imported New Zealand cheese from the Royal Docks in London. These were brought to the cold stores at Crown Quay at Sittingbourne because of a lack of cold store space in London. There were two large Cheddar cheeses to each of the crates. Apparently, some local entrepreneurs got into trouble when they found a way to slice open a cheese, scoop out a large piece and reseal it. At the time cheese was still rationed and it must have been a temptation.

Processed hoofs and horns were loaded at the Royal Primrose Soap works at Silvertown and taken to the Agrigano mill at Faversham where they were steamed and ground to make hoof and horn meal. It was a smelly business. The discharging took place in the dock at the top end of the creek.

Occasionally, sub-let cargoes of coal from Purfleet to C. Townsend Hook and Co. Ltd. at Snodland were obtained from the London and Rochester Trading Co. Ltd. who held the contract. Tony Lapthorn and Stan Yeates both piloted ships, usually Dutch, to Snodland with coal or china clay and also to Reeds Paper Mill at Aylesford. One ship, the *Corsica* (242/1940), regularly took wood pulp to Reeds and then reloaded waste paper. This work was generally obtained through the broker Mr Thompson of Watson and Gill at Rochester. A trip to Reeds had other attractions because a good meal could be had very cheaply at the subsidised works canteen.

Beech boles were a fairly regular cargo for several years. These were huge beech logs, sawn into planks and banded. Being very heavy and difficult to stow, the bands would often burst and the planks had to be restacked. They were loaded in France at Dieppe, Le Treport and Fecamp or along the Seine at La Mailleraye. The cargo was taken to Corporation Quay at Southend-on-Sea or Burtons Wharf at Gillingham. Apparently, the nature of the fibrous composition of French beech made it a superior timber for furniture making because it was better at holding upholstery tacks than British beech. The timber was also used for making coffins.

Foundry sand was loaded at Patmans Wharf at Upnor for Fords at Dagenham. Cullet was also loaded at Patmans for the glass works at Zeebrugge and after discharge the ship would drop down to a French port for a return cargo of beech boles. A skipper would be paid £20 for the round voyage and, with luck, he could do two voyages a week. Similar voyages involved loading flints at St.Valery sur Somme. Other regular work came through Rye Shipping Ltd. when the ships loaded grain and horse beans at the Town Quay at Rye for Rotterdam.

More motor ships
An elderly former Dutch coaster, the *Herb*, was purchased in 1962 and renamed *Hoocreek* (1). She pioneered the company's continental trading. One of her first voyages was from Deptford Creek to Brussels with a cargo of baled waste paper. Life does not always run smoothly and she once had an embarrassment when caught in heavy weather off Dover. She was on a light passage and was pounding so badly that the crew thought she was breaking up and abandoned ship. Compared with later ships her water ballast capacity was meagre, no double bottoms, just a tiny forepeak and an afterpeak. The engine had been left running and the ship went around in circles until she was taken in tow by a Dutch tug. The underwriters paid the ensuing salvage claim and returned the ship to the

Hoocreek (1). *[Company archives]*

company. As another claim to fame, she was the first *Hoo* ship to venture as far as Teignmouth when she arrived there under the command of John Chancellor.

Mary Birch joined the company's continental trading for a while in 1964 but soon reverted to the ballast trade. Her cubic capacity had been reduced when the bulkheads were fitted for the ballast work making her unsuitable for many cargoes except perhaps cullet and flints. Purchased in 1959, *Yarvic*, originally a wartime VIC lighter, ventured to the continent but also carried her share of ballast. *Raycreek*, another elderly former Dutch coaster, was purchased in 1960. After three years' service she experienced a serious engine problem and was derated to a barge; used for china clay she was loaded at Ridham Dock and towed around to the mill at Kemsley. When the work tailed off she was taken to Hoo and broken up.

The motor barges and these early motor ships were all below 300 gross tons which was the threshold of the Radio Convention and were not legally required to carry radiotelephones. It does seem strange today, with the present plethora of communication equipment, that these ships had nothing. They had distress rockets and flares or

Above: *Hoocrest* (1). *[Company archives]*

Opposite top: *Hoopride* (1) at Jersey. *[D. Hocquard]*

Opposite bottom: *Hoopride* (1) at sea in 1982. *[C. Reynolds]*

Below: *Hootact*. *[C. Reynolds collection]*

made their own signals by burning oil soaked rags or blankets as a last resort. If they urgently needed to contact the company the only options were through the kindness of another ship or to put in somewhere and use a telephone.

W.W. Burton Ltd.
This company was a coal merchant and operated the business from Gillingham Pier which, as a private venture, was purchased by Tony and Rachel Lapthorn in 1967. The coal business was stopped and they built a warehouse and grain silo on the site. Many ships were loaded at the pier including shipments of locally grown barley. During 1974, the premises were sold to AKZO (UK) Ltd., the British subsidiary of the Dutch chemical company and much of the capital raised was eventually used to buy back the Lapthorn shares held by Gaselee (qv). The balance of the money went towards the purchase of the *Hoopride* (1)(460/1957). The ship was owned jointly with LJT Shipping Ltd. who held 11/64 of the shares.

Sailing
No doubt as a form of relief from all the day to day trials and tribulations of running a shipping company, Tony indulged his love of sailing by being skipper of Walter Brice's sailing barges *Ardeer* and *Spinaway C* in the annual Medway and Pin Mill Sailing Barge Matches. He won one of these and his son David, a crew member, recalls that they were kept at their stations and forbidden any food until they had won the race. The barges also undertook charter cruises on the UK coast and to the continent but Stan Yeates was usually asked to take command for these. Stan Yeates, John Chancellor and others at Hoo were frequently involved in re-rigging sailing craft, in particular spritsail barges for various owners.

Spinaway C. [T. Farnham collection]

Reorganization

The relationship with Gaselee continued until Gaselee and Son (Felixstowe) Ltd., the last remaining part of the towage business, was sold and became Alexandra Towing Co. (Felixstowe) Ltd. in 1975. Gaselee had intended their Felixstowe operation to capitalise on the growing container trade into the port but had to concede that they did not have the resources to compete as the container ships increased in size. Alexandra did not want the complication of a shipping company included in the deal and insisted that the Lapthorn shares were sold. Tony and Rachel Lapthorn had recently sold some assets - Gillingham Pier belonging to their jointly owned W.W. Burton Ltd. (*qv*) - and were able to buy back half of the Gaselee 60% shareholding in the company. The remaining 30% were split equally between the two Gaselee directors on the Lapthorn board, Dick Hazell and Auriol Gaselee. The shareholding now became:

Lapthorn family	40%
W.W. Burton Ltd.	30%
Dick Hazell	15%
Auriol Gaselee	15%.

A little later, in 1978, the remaining 30% of shares were purchased and the holdings became:

Lapthorn family	49%.
W.W. Burton Ltd.	51%.

This was not considered to be an ideal situation and in 1984, W.W. Burton Ltd. was restructured becoming R. Lapthorn and Co. (Holdings) Ltd., at the same time acquiring the 49% shareholding from the family. In part, this was financed from the proceeds of the sale of the *Hoopride* (1). R. Lapthorn and Co. (Holdings) Ltd. thus became and remains the controlling company for all the others in the group.

Towage 2

The tug *Hooligan* was involved in a number of interesting and exciting tows in addition to the salvage of the *Lune Fisher* previously described. On another occasion the tug went to the assistance of the *Hoocreek* whose engine had broken down during heavy weather in the English Channel. It had taken some time to get the tug mobilised and by the time Tony and Stan Yeates got under way the weather had started to moderate. Nevertheless, there was still a heavy swell running to make things difficult. Two runs were made to leeward of the ship but they failed to pass a line. The next run was made more slowly and Stan managed to get a heaving line aboard the ship although the hand who caught it seemed not to be making much of an effort and got some words for his dilatory performance. It was not until later that it was discovered that he had taken the monkey's fist full on the face and had a black eye, cuts and bruises to show for it. The ship was finally made fast and towed, with her cargo of beech boles, into Ramsgate.

The *Hooligan* was also used to tow loaded lighters on sea passages and once went to Portsmouth with a big double length lighter to load a large GRP craft destined for export and exhibition in America. It was loaded and secured when a Board of Trade surveyor arrived and insisted on a loadline survey and hatch coverings for the unmanned lighter. This was thought to be impractical and unnecessary but the official insisted and also wanted the forepeak hatch on the lighter welded shut. The misunderstandings were probably due to a combination of the company being more conversant with estuarial and river work coupled with an over zealous surveyor. The work took several days and eventually, in deteriorating weather, they were allowed to sail complete with a loadline painted on the lighter. The engine misbehaved on passage and they just managed to get into Newhaven on Saturday night. The skipper, Stan Yeates, telephoned Tony, who located a similar engine, rushed it to Newhaven where it was fitted and they were able to sail again on Sunday evening. It was imperative to get the cargo to London for the big ship to load it and sail on Tuesday. It was certainly touch and go but the deadline was kept.

Hooligan was eventually sold to the Acorn Shipyard and renamed *Acorn*. She was kept for a few years before being broken up.

Hoocreek (1) aground in Faversham Creek. *[C. Traill]*

Warehousing
Always on the lookout for a good business opportunity, Tony and Rachel Lapthorn went into partnership with Walter Brice and formed Brice and Lapthorn Ltd. in 1965. Two large warehouses were built at Hoo; the company name was painted on the sides in large letters and could be seen for miles. A number of commodities including bags of haricot beans and similar produce were stored in the warehouses. The business succeeded reasonably well but when the partners received a good offer they decided to sell. The warehouses are still in existence. The builder, Site-Cast Ltd., was a local specialist in pre-cast concrete buildings and had produced the first airport buildings for Alderney. The prefabricated sections were loaded over the wharf at Hoo for shipment to the island.

Acorn Shipyard Ltd.
The small repair yard and grid, situated on the Rochester side of Bridge Reach and approached on the land side from Gashouse Road, was regularly used by many coastal vessels including those of Lapthorn and Union Transport (London) Ltd. P & O had acquired the yard, previously owned by the New Medway Steam Packet Co. Ltd., through their subsidiary, General Steam Navigation Co. Ltd. It no longer fitted in with any of their operations and they had decided to sell. One evening in 1977 at one of the shipping industry dinners, Tony Lapthorn was returning in the lift to his hotel room when he met Max Heinimann, chairman of Union Transport (London) Ltd. Tony suggested that they made a joint purchase. Max was interested and they spoke again the next day and decided to go ahead. Preparation of the sale agreement was a protracted affair and after six weeks of discussion no agreement was in sight. In the end, a simple cash deal to purchase land, buildings and assets was structured, whereupon, Lapthorn and Union Transport became the joint owners.

The contemporary ships of both owners were generally not in the first flush of youth and required more frequent slipping and repairs than might newer vessels. Some of the slippings could be of an emergency nature and it made sense to have priority at a yard in the Medway. The yard was therefore kept quite busy with the owners' work. As the two principals bought newer ships the pattern began to change and much of the work now involved outsiders. This made some money for the partners but in 1986 it was decided to sell the Lapthorn shares to Union Transport who thus became the sole owner.

The fleet expands
A number of small but more modern motor ships joined the fleet in the late 1960s and early 1970s. The first of these was the *Hoofinch*, initially taken on bareboat charter from Springwell Shipping Ltd. whose owner, Francis P. Longton, was disposing of his shipping interests to retire and concentrate on his horses. The ship was purchased outright some ten years later.

Most of the others were between ten and twenty years old when purchased and were really the only type of ships available and affordable at the time. They joined the earlier ships in the developing continental and Channel Island trade. Between them they firmly established not only the company's reputation for smart and well-kept ships but also the naming style started in jocular fashion with the little tug *Hooray*.

They were *Hootact*, *Hoocrest*, *Hootern*, *Hoopride*, *Hoofort* and a few years later the good-looking *Hoomoss*. Apart from the *Hoofort*, built at Troon as the *Ramsey*, they were all Dutch-built and owned. Nearly all the names have been used again for later ships although in some cases split into two words. Most of these early ships had grey upperworks above an accentuated black boot topping.

The *Hoocrest* achieved a little local notoriety, although it has to be said that it occurred after the company had sold her. She lay at Queenborough in a deteriorating condition and although reported to have been renamed *Atlantic Comet* it is doubtful if this actually took place. Indeed, quite coincidentally, the manager of the local scrap

Hoofinch (1) loading at Rye. *[Company archives]*

Hoomoss (1) at St.Malo. *[C. Reynolds]*

merchants was asked to affirm to the Registrar that she was no longer in a seagoing condition in order that the name *Hoocrest* could be used again by Lapthorn in 1986. This indicates that the register had not been closed or the name officially changed. The company had received a phone call from H.M. Immigration Service asking them to comment on the number of crew members that the ship might carry. They were aghast to learn that the true complement could be as low as six or seven men. It seems that the ship's name had been used by someone to bring many illegal immigrants, posing as crew members, into this country from the continent. She was latterly cut down for use as a floating dock for small craft and rather embarrassingly now lies at Hoo with her original name clearly showing.

Hootern was not owned but was arguably the first ship to be fully managed for another owner. This statement does not contradict the claim of *Gladys* or *Peterna* because in both these cases the management only extended to commercial matters and perhaps technical expertise and resources as required. The ship, as the *Dolphin City*, was owned by City of London Tankers Ltd., and was renamed when the management commenced. The owner was a partner in a firm of London marine solicitors. The company retained the management when the vessel was sold to General Freight Co. Ltd. two years later and was renamed *River Taw*. In 1979 she damaged her bottom at Briton Ferry and became a constructive total loss. She was later sold and repaired for further trading in the Caribbean.

Hoocrest (1) loading stone at Dean Quarry. *[C. Reynolds collection]*

Left: *Hootact*. [D. Hocquard]

Below: *Hoofort* (1). [C. Hill]

Hoocrest spent some time on time charter to LJT Shipping Ltd., whose principal, Laurie J. Thompson, had sub-let her to General Freight for the soya meal trade from Erith to Selby. Laurie Thompson had worked for the shipbrokers Such and Schooley Ltd. who had handled all the chartering for Metcalf Motor Coasters Ltd. until they were taken over by Booker Brothers Ltd. At that time he set up on his own and was involved with many coastal shipping companies but in particular he handled all the chartering for Weston Shipping.

In 1974, Weston Shipping were looking for a Dutch ship for the grain trade from the French bay. Tony Lapthorn heard from Laurie Thompson that they had considered the *Berend N* as a good, sound ship but had turned her down in favour of something a little larger. He inspected the ship and decided to buy her. W.W. Burton Ltd. and LJT Shipping Ltd., who took 11 of the 64 shares, jointly purchased the ship that was renamed *Hoopride*. The ship had been built and owned by one or another of the companies in the Niestern group of Delfzijl although at the time of purchase the manager had become D. Davids and Zoon, also of Delfzijl.

These slightly larger ships were all above the convention 300 gross tons and therefore carried radiotelephones to enable them to communicate directly with the company and their agents while still at sea. Times were changing and the expectations of people, ashore and afloat soon made it necessary to fit VHF radiotelephones and radar sets to keep pace with developments. The VHFs made communications in coastal waters and in port so much easier that it soon became difficult to imagine life without them. In the 1960s and early 1970s the use of radar was still a controversial subject and seen merely as an aid to navigation, it definitely ranked behind a visual lookout usually described as the 'Mark 1 Eyeball'. The company started to fit radar sets in 1968 and the crews paid the rental from their share.

Gebert Shipping Ltd.

In 1976, Lapthorn became involved with Gebert Shipping Ltd. of Jersey in the management of their two ships, *Delta-G* and *Argo-G*. Both ships were registered in Jersey. The owners, Albert Davids, the son of D. Davids of Delfzijl and his wife Geissen, were friends of Tony Lapthorn.

These two ships created their own little difficulties in a surprising way. Lapthorns were founder members in 1978 of the Small Ships Training Group (SSTG), an organisation set up to train officers and ratings on non-federated British ships with the assistance of grants from the British government. The legal situation with trainees on ships with other than a plain Red Ensign was, to say the least, unclear. At the time it was considered that the trainees were not eligible for any grant aid but in later years a more enlightened principle emerged and grants were paid to British trainees whatever the flag of their ship provided that their employing company or training provider was British. At the time, with the exception of bona fide Channel Islands or Manx-owned vessels, flags of open or off-shore registers had not really arrived in the UK coastal trades to any great extent and these two Jersey flag ships caused quite a stir.

Management of the *Delta-G* ceased in 1983 when she was sold. Management of the *Argo-G* lasted another year until she was sold to joint owners Lapthorn and Jacobs and Tenvig (Offshore) Ltd. who needed a short-term tax vehicle. From photographs it is quite clear that there is a hyphen in *Delta-G* whereas there is a full stop in *Argo-G*. *Lloyd's Register* shows both to be hyphens and this is the correct situation. The discrepancy was probably down to the sailors and their paintbrushes.

Tony Lapthorn had a little excitement in connection with the Davids when he was helping Mrs. Davids to clear up her husband's shipping affairs in Holland after his death. For his own business he had picked up a windlass gypsy from the Ten Horn factory and put it in the boot of Mrs. Davids' car. When they crossed the border into Belgium they were met with a zealous customs official who searched the car and could not help finding the gypsy. It had not been declared, nor did they have the requisite 'T' form to export the equipment. It all became a little confused and acrimonious with Tony insisting it was a gypsy for a British ship but when Mrs. Davids described it as a flower pot, the customs man dug in his heels. His superior was summoned and soon assessed the situation. Tony was told to go to the next border crossing where 'T' forms would be available but in the event he was waved through and heard no more.

Above: *Delta-G*.
 [Company archives]

Right: *Argo-G*. [C. Hill]

Wiggs. [Company archives]

Eggar, Forrester (Holdings) Ltd.
After reading articles in the technical press about some simple twin-screw canal craft built by The Yorkshire Dry Dock Co. Ltd. at Hull, John Golding, a manager at Eggar, Forrester made further enquiries. He undertook a short trial trip and following further discussions with the builder he was convinced that, suitably modified for seagoing employment, these small craft would make ideal coastal cargo vessels. After protracted negotiations, his company ordered three of the ships and before the first, *Wilks*, was delivered in 1976 he had invited Lapthorn to become the technical and personnel manager. The masters were all former Eggar, Forrester employees having served in their previous fleet of coastal vessels. The company was also requested to take over the chartering management whenever John Golding was on holiday or otherwise engaged.

These Yorkshire Dry Dock standard twin-screw coasters, or YDD boxes as they were colloquially known, broke new ground in many ways, not least the manning. John Golding and David Lapthorn had discussions with the Government about manning in general but particularly about the engine power. They maintained that only the power of one engine should be taken into account and as this would be below the convention kilowatt breakpoint, there was no requirement for an engineer. This was not totally accepted but a compromise was reached whereby the ships could trade in a restricted area with four men. The Government officials had their own agenda and, whatever the rights or wrongs of John Golding's case, or what they thought privately, the officials felt they had to bear in mind the effect such a precedent could have on the much more powerful twin-engined off-shore supply ships.

Wiris on the slipway at Denton. [Author]

Before the third vessel had been delivered from Hull, Eggar, Forrester had already placed an order with a Danish shipbuilder for three very similar but cheaper ships. Lapthorn also managed this second group of ships. The Danish trio departed from the very basic design concept by having double bottom ballast tanks and other equipment. They were thus more sophisticated than the original YDD ships whose very simplicity had attracted John Golding, who thought that coastal trading could be efficiently carried out by the simplest of ships. This may be true but it depends how far the principle is taken because it is also true that ships without a reasonable ballast capacity are prone to uneconomic weather delays and damage, particularly in north west European waters. The balance between the one and the other is of necessity a compromise.

The operation of these six ships, quite unlike any others in the company's fleet at the time, provided the necessary experience for much of what was to come later. There was a steep learning curve for shore and sea staff during the early voyages when dedication and ingenuity was required to overcome the teething problems. Eventually, most of the particular difficulties of the machinery and equipment were smoothed out and the more unrealistic expectations of charterers assuaged.

By 1984, the management of Eggar, Forrester was concerned about a potential conflict of interests with Lapthorn who now had similar ships of their own. They were also concerned about their cash-flow situation and determined to curtail some of the outflow by managing their own ships. This was seen as having the benefit of putting more work and income into their Tilbury office that had been in danger of closing. The management of the six ships was then taken away from Lapthorn and attempts made to manage them 'in house'. The result was not very good and after a few months it was decided to sell the ships but in the meantime they were given to another coastal company, F.T. Everard and Sons Ltd. to manage while buyers were found and the office in Tilbury closed.

David A. Lapthorn

David was born in Bournemouth in 1948 at the time his father Tony was becoming established as a manager at the Whitewall boatyard at Frindsbury. The family home became the sailing barge *Leslie* moored in Whitewall Creek but later moved to the Hoo Marina. Later, the *Leslie* was sold and the family moved into the larger *Alice May*. David attended the local village school at Hoo and can remember the move of the *Alice May* from the marina to Buttercrock Wharf when he and his classmates walked down to the wharf to see the rather unusual house move. He later went to Sevenoaks School and left in 1967.

There was never any real doubt that he would work in his father's business and a training period was arranged with friendly companies to prepare him for the future. First he went to J.W. Cook and Co. (Wivenhoe) Ltd. who had recently built ships for the company. Here he spent three months in each of the workshops although he admits to cutting short his stint in the paint shop. Having gained basic experience in ship construction he went on to Colchester in December 1968 to work with W. Fieldgate and Son Ltd. to learn about shipbroking and agency work.

He returned to Hoo in June 1970 and while still studying for the examinations of the Institute of Chartered Shipbrokers, he worked, mainly in the chartering department but also turning his hand to anything that was required, as is the way of a family company. He was elected to the board of the company on 4th December 1974 when, having passed the examinations, he became a Fellow of the Institute of Chartered Shipbrokers (FICS).

David became the Managing Director on 6th June 1981, his father Tony's sixtieth birthday. On that day he handed the company's chartering to a competent chartering manager and wondered what to do in his new position. For some while he had been thinking about the current fleet and the future. The fleet comprised eleven ships of which seven were managed for other owners. It was clear that some new ships were needed if the company was to survive

David A. Lapthorn. *[Company archives]*

and develop. Margins were small and the cost of new ships and the cost of loans to finance them were high, making it difficult to see the way ahead. David knew that many shipyards were as keen to obtain orders as he was to obtain new ships and thought that the two desires could be brought together to their mutual advantage. Adopting the old adage that nothing ventured is nothing gained, he wrote to three British shipyards suggesting that they might consider participating in a joint building and operating deal to reduce the current financial burdens of both. One company failed to reply, Cooks answered that, regretfully, they were unable to enter into such an arrangement but The Yorkshire Dry Dock Co. Ltd. answered favourably and suggested an early meeting to discuss the matter.

John H. Whitaker (Holdings) Ltd.
The parent company of the shipbuilder, itself a shipowner, was most anxious to recoup some recent investment at the yard and the letter from David Lapthorn seemed to offer the best available opportunity. After some discussion, a joint equity deal and a specification for a ship was agreed between the companies. The ship, *Hoo Venture*, was built in 1982 and was owned jointly by R. Lapthorn and Co. Ltd. and John H. Whitaker (Holdings) Ltd. Finance was arranged through the National Westminster Bank with a fixed rate of interest according to the contemporary Government regulations for shipbuilding support. The company bought the Whitaker share in 1995 and thus became the sole owner.

Whitakers built three more ships for their own account, *Whitonia*, *Betty-Jean* and *Bowcliffe*, all being given to the company to manage. *Betty-Jean* and *Bowcliffe* were jointly owned with Bayford and Co. Ltd. of Leeds, an oil supplier in the area and closely associated with Whitakers. The three ships remained under the management of the company with the exception of a short period when *Whitonia* was bareboat chartered to Apollo Ships Ltd. of Rochford. Later, *Whitonia* (renamed *Antonia B*) and *Betty-Jean* were bareboat chartered jointly to Lapthorn and Byron Chartering and Trading Co. Ltd. of Chelmsford. The company became the sole charterer when Byron went into voluntary liquidation in 1999. As things turned out, interest and capital repayments became less than the charter hire and the ships were purchased in 1999 becoming *Hoofort* and *Hoomoss* respectively. *Bowcliffe* was renamed *Fast Ken* for the duration of a time charter to Fastlines of Antwerp but the management, as far as technical and personnel matters were concerned, remained with the company. The ship reverted to her original name at the end of the charter in 1999.

Although the shipyard has now been sold and the management input has much reduced, the close contacts built up over the years between Lapthorn and Whitaker still remain.

John I. Jacobs PLC
To diversify from their traditional tanker business, John I. Jacobs had settled on the idea of building two passenger launches to be operated on demise charter to George Wheeler Launches Ltd. on the Thames. The launches were designed by Ernest C. Wilson of Gravesend and ordered from the Bideford Shipyard in Devon. They were to have traditional Jacobs' names; *Rosewood* and *Hollywood*. The first was laid down but before she could be launched the yard went into receivership leaving the ship on the slip. Yorkshire Dry Dock purchased the ship from the liquidator, cut it into sections and took it to Hull to be reassembled and completed as their yard number 267. The order for the second craft was maintained and as yard number 273 was completed in 1981. Ernest Wilson kept his interest in the craft and produced all the drawings.

The two river launches became the catalysts for other developments. Donald Beveridge, the manager of the Yorkshire Dry Dock, spoke to John I. Jacobs about the small ships he had built for Eggar, Forrester and also the joint deal that was progressing between Lapthorn and his principals. John I. Jacobs was quite keen to invest in coasters and to obtain the investment grants currently

Hoo Venture. [C. Reynolds]

Bowcliffe. [Fotoflite]

available. The choice of manager naturally fell on Lapthorn. The ownership was purely a financial arrangement and, as Jacobs wished to distance themselves from the operation of the ships, they forbore to use their traditional ship names and instead opted for the *Hoo* names and the colours of their manager.

The association with Jacobs was to dominate the company's activities for nearly twenty years and from a fleet of about a dozen small and elderly ships, within twelve years it was to become the largest fleet of modern dry cargo coasters in the United Kingdom. It was also a success story for Yorkshire Dry Dock because with series production and a long order book, not only with ships for Jacobs, they were able to reduce their costs and remain competitive.

The first of the coasters built for Jacobs was *Hoocreek*, yard number 278, completed in 1982. The name was only one word indicating that the managers operated the ship on a fixed bareboat charter with a terminal purchase option. Other ships had two-word names, e.g. *Hoo Plover* and *Hoo Willow*, indicating a different basis for the payment of net freight or management fees although there was a bareboat charter element in all of them. The distinction between one and two word names was not an infallible guide because with at least one ship the builders misunderstood the instructions and a ship emerged with one word when it should have been two.

Various Jacobs' group companies became involved with the ships, starting with John I. Jacobs PLC in 1984, Jacobs and Tenvig (Offshore) Ltd. about 1985; the latter becoming Jacobs Offshore Ltd. in 1991 and dropping out altogether when the offshore company was sold to Seascope PLC later in the same year. Jacobs and Partners Ltd. came on the scene about 1986. The choice of names fell into a general pattern; ships owned by John I. Jacobs had tree names, e.g. *Hoo Laurel,* large bird names initially indicated that Tenvig was involved, e.g., *Hoo Swan*. Later

Rosewood. [Company archives]

Hoocreek (2). [C. Hill]

it indicated that Lapthorn was a joint owner, e.g. *Hoo Falcon*. Small bird names, e.g. *Hoo Robin*, indicated that Lapthorn was a joint owner with Jacobs and Partners. Fish names, e.g. *Hoo Dolphin*, indicated that Jacobs and Partners were the sole owners.

From 1989 five of the ships had slightly different ownership arrangements although they were the same as all the others from an operational standpoint. *Hoo Swan, Hoo Finch, Hoo Swift, Hoo Falcon* and *Hoo Kestrel* were owned jointly by Jacobs and R. Lapthorn and Co. Ltd. but bareboat chartered to R. Lapthorn (Holdings) Ltd. The bareboat charter remained until R. Lapthorn and Co. Ltd. became the sole owner in 1996.

At the Annual General Meeting of John I. Jacobs PLC in 1994, the chairman Mr J.H. Jacobs retired and Michael Kingshott was appointed chief executive. He already owned about 25% of Jacobs' shares and had plans for the future. The ships were all transferred to the ownership of Jacobs VI Ltd., specially formed in 1994 for the purpose. He was very critical of the coasters' performance and had decided that he could do more with the capital tied up in them. In 1995 a complicated deal was arranged and the company acquired the Jacobs' interests in all 17 ships for £10.5 million spread over several years. The initial payment was £5.3 million, a further £2.5 million between 1999 and 2004, while the remaining £2.7 million is debt related to UK shipping support.

After the purchase, Jacobs VI Ltd. became R. Lapthorn Shipping Ltd. To tidy things, the ships were transferred to the ownership of R. Lapthorn and Co. Ltd. in 1996. Although the company is now the sole owner of all the ships, there is no move to standardise the names and reduce them all to one word. There is quite a cost implication for little reward and in any event the difference now seems largely irrelevant.

In a press release at the time of the acquisition in July 1995, David Lapthorn sought to counter the criticism of the ships' performance and stated 'Our company performance is as keen as any competitor; it is the sector that is under performing not the company. The main thing with the enlarged fleet is that we can determine our own level of satisfaction'.

Yorkshire Dry Dock twin-screw coasters

From the *Hoo Venture* of 1982, these ships developed in terms of size and sophistication without departing too far from the original concept of frugality, modified in the light of experience, contemporary expectations, regulations and equipment. During the building programme there was a constant dialogue between the company and the builder with suggestions for improvements based on the operational experience of both. Tony Lapthorn himself acted as the owner's superintendent and closely scrutinised all stages of the construction.

Although the shipyard tended to think of them in classes according to their length - 50, 58 and 78 metres - the company naturally classes them in terms of their approximate deadweight tonnage; 1,100, 1,300 and 2,000. These classifications cut right through the naming sequences that have no relevance in this context; nor for that matter in any other now that the company owns all of them.

The *Wilks* and her sisters were powered by two Caterpillar six-cylinder D343 or on the later ships, 8-cylinder D3408 engines driving Aquamaster 400 azimuthing propeller units. These were found to be operating on their limits and consequently had a poor maintenance record. The more powerful Cummins KT1150-M engines improved on this performance and

Cummins KT19-M marine engine. [Cummins Engine Co. Ltd.]

Hoo Maple shortly after launching, with another ship under construction in the background. *[C. Reynolds]*

were fitted to the 1,100 ton class and to the early ships of the 1,300 ton class. The KT19-M engines followed and were themselves superseded by the later KTA19-M units complete with fitted aftercoolers. There was little difference between the KT1150 and KT19 units and the numbers were merely two ways of identifying the same engine capacity; 1,150 cubic inches or 19 litres.

The first fourteen ships, from *Hoo Venture* in 1982 to *Hoocrest* in 1986, had the Aquamaster 401 units. The next group of five ships, *Hoo Finch* of 1988 to *Hoo Beech* of 1989, had the smaller Aquamaster 381 units but these were later replaced by 601 units similar to those already installed in the final group of ships. It was found that the larger 601 units provided the best balance. The combination of the larger engines and Aquamaster units, working within their limits, made for better reliability and efficiency.

Although *Lloyd's Register* states that the KT1150-M, KT19-M and KTA19-M 'in line' engines were made in various places - Columbus, Charleston and Daventry - it is most likely that they were all made in Seymour, Indiana with certification coming from the Charleston office. The confusion probably arises from letters and other documents coming from the Columbus office. In the case of the

Ilona G with masts lowered off Northfleet. *[C. Reynolds]*

Anna Maria at Goole. *[C. Hill]*

Daventry engines it could simply mean that the aftercoolers were fitted or some other modification carried out there before the engines were delivered to the shipyard.

The hull form of the early ships was tank tested in the Wolfson Unit at Southampton University and improvements made to the lines of the *Hoo Venture* and later ships. The ships' holds were also subject to continuing development. To facilitate cargo operations it is necessary to have the largest possible opening with the minimum of obstructions. As the ships became longer, this became more difficult to achieve and it was thought necessary to fit a portable beam at the mid-length. Frames were strengthened and the single-hold and hatch configuration was retained. Although some of the company's early ships were registered at Rochester, the *Hoo Venture* was registered at Hull being part owned by Whitakers; later ships, owned wholly or in part by one of the Jacobs companies, were registered in London. The Lapthorn and Jacobs ships were all painted in the standard colours of white upperworks, black hull with a bow badge of a yellow star and red boottopping.

Towards the end of the twin-screw coaster programme, in 1990/91, a single-screw vessel, *Ilona G*, was built for Harris and Dixon (Shipbrokers) Ltd. They declined to take up their option on a second vessel and the order was transferred to an associated client company, Beulah Shipping Ltd., and completed as the *Anna Maria*. These single-screw ships had Cummins KTA19-M vee form engines made at Daventry. The company initially carried out the management for both vessels but later that year the Dutch financier of the *Anna Maria* became a little uneasy at having both a British owner and manager and insisted on the appointment of a Dutch manager. The new manager put the vessel to work on his normal cargoes and she was soon trading to the Mediterranean. In 1994 the company bought the ship and she was renamed *Anna Meryl* for David Lapthorn's wife. The company has had close relations for many years with Harris and Dixon and the managing director John Churchward who was also associated with Beulah Shipping Ltd. and Byron Chartering and Trading Co. Ltd. Both Harris and Dixon and Byron have been involved in bareboat charters of the ships from time to time.

Hoo Kestrel, last ship of the Yorkshire Dry Dock series. *[C. Reynolds]*

The building programme was concluded with the 2,000 ton class and the final ship, *Hoo Kestrel*, came into service in 1993. During the eleven years, starting with the *Hoo Venture* of 1982, the company was involved in the building of no less than twenty-five ships. This was certainly no mean achievement.

As built, these ships had the standard MF and VHF radio telephones for communications but when the new Global Marine Distress and Safety System (GMDSS) came into operation the MF radios had to be replaced with equipment capable of working the new system. At the same time, cellular phones were fitted to provide good, secure communications whenever a ship is in range of an aerial.

Other ships for management
As if the flood of ships coming from Yorkshire Dry Dock was not enough to cope with, the company also briefly managed some other ships. The *Ellen W* and *Freda W* formed an interesting pair. They had originally been ordered by Mardorf Peach and Co. Ltd. but had been demise chartered for fifteen years to the Unilever Group company, BOCM Silcock Ltd., although the technical and personnel management was carried out by Weston Shipping. They were named after two of the charterer's directors. Eight years into the demise charter, BOCM Silcock acquired the ships but the management arrangements were continued. The freight managers had always been another Unilever Group company, General Freight Co. Ltd.

General Freight was one of the biggest charterers of coastal shipping having the responsibility for arranging the water transport of all the group's massive tonnage of oil seeds, oil cake, grains, meal, edible oil and other commodities. From this position they could see that the crew costs of a federated ship were much higher than those of a similar non-federated ship. Defederating a ship was still quite a step to take at the time and had to be carefully considered. To reduce the risks, the ships were laid up for a while, sold to another Unilever Group company and then renamed. General Freight looked around for a non-federated manager and chose Lapthorn in 1982. This arrangement lasted for two years until the management was transferred to G.T. Gillie and Blair Ltd. of Newcastle-on-Tyne shortly before the ships were sold. The ships have changed hands several times since then but are still in operation.

At much the same time the company was also involved in the management of several elderly vessels. This ranged from freight management or technical management or both and, in one case, a commitment to provide technical services if requested. Such loose and informal arrangements were quite common at the time but have more or less disappeared in today's more regulated world. Brian Cuckow of Gillingham owned two of the ships, *Nautic W* and *Sellina C*. Coincidentally, several changes of name and ownership later, both sank in 1991. Others were the *Gieny S* and *Rover T,* both owned by Medway-based companies. Harris and Dixon purchased the *Finlandia* in 1985 to facilitate the acquisition of the new *Dowlais*. During the period the ship was renamed *Mary Coast* and eventually sold to D.J. Goubert Shipping Ltd. of Guernsey. Much later, in 1998, there was another short-term management arrangement when the company managed the *Nicky L* for Waveney Shipping 2 PLC.

Wider trading
With the ever-growing fleet it became necessary to look for a wider range of cargoes. Although the early basics of ballast, cement, fertilisers, beech boles and others remained, the company had to look for other cargoes to keep the ships occupied and, crucial to a profitable operation, to obtain return cargoes to keep light passages to a minimum. Over the years the company ships have carried the whole range of coastal cargoes and in addition to those mentioned above can be included, grain, meal, bricks, tiles, steel coils, plates and billets, explosives and munitions, coal, slag and many more.

At first, due to the manning and certification regulations, the ships were confined to the British Home Trade area also known as the Elbe-Brest Limits. This area extended all around the British Isles to Brest in the south west and the river Elbe in the north east. These were well-known rules but they did create much dissatisfaction and frustration amongst British owners. Taking an extreme example with a ship sailing from Lerwick to Hamburg; why could she not enter a Danish port like Ebsjerg when she had

Freda W. [C. Hill]

Hoo Marlin in the Thames. *[Company archives]*

to pass the place anyway? Why, having got to the entrance of the Elbe, could she not pass through the canal to Kiel? It was particularly galling for the company and other British owners to see similar ships of other flags taking advantage of apparently much wider and more flexible trading limits.

Eventually the British limits were extended to Cape St. Vincent in the south west, to Bergen on the Norwegian coast and including the Baltic Sea apart from a seasonal exclusion beyond Kalmar in the winter. This gave the chartering department much wider options in the quest for cargoes and the development of new trades. But they are always hard people to satisfy and within days of the new limits entering into force they were asking if it were possible to ' just pop around the corner' at Cape St. Vincent and load a cargo in Huelva!

In the early days, most of the crews lived close to the Essex or Suffolk rivers where ballast was loaded or the Kent rivers where it was discharged. These seafarers were generally former sailing barge men, without official certificates, but well qualified by practical experience. They graduated to the early motorships and with the company they grew into the wider coastal and continental trades. The development of these trades presented the company with a potential problem because when the Government, stimulated by the international convention of 1978, introduced the new certificate structure in 1980, all watchkeeping officers were required to hold certificates.

As an interim measure, all existing officers, whether certificated or not, provided they could pass an eyesight test, were granted a certificate of service to enable them to continue. The problem related to the next step because to be promoted, an officer was required to hold the certificate of competency for the higher position. This could only be acquired by passing examinations. It was no longer possible, in the time-honoured fashion, to promote a promising sailor to mate or a good mate to master.

Another international convention, this time in 1995, refined the certificate structure and trading limits making the task of management even more difficult. Traditional sources of recruitment have long since vanished and the company now relies heavily on direct recruitment and the training of young seafarers using the programmes developed by the SSTG. Unfortunately, these do not provide sufficient British seafarers and, in common with many other coastal employers, the company has recently resorted to recruiting foreign officers and ratings.

Later developments
Right from the earliest days the company has maintained some engineering facilities at Hoo but in 1989 it became associated with a marine engineering company at Goole and L & M Engineers Ltd. was formed on a 50/50 basis in 1991. The existing company workshops at Hoo became part of the new venture and John Lapthorn, Tony's third son and an engineer, became the managing director. In 1995 the company shareholding was increased to 75/25. Another depot was opened at Par in Cornwall giving the company virtually nation wide coverage of the major coastal trading areas. In a separate venture, a new company, L & M Shipyards Ltd. leased Denton Slipway at Gravesend during 2000 to provide a slipway for craft up to about 1,000 tons and repair facilities on the Thames. The two engineering companies deal with voyage repairs and dockings, overhauls of main and auxiliary machinery and make a speciality of high pressure water blasting.

In 1991, the company purchased Kodde Shipping and Trading BV., the Rotterdam-based agency and shipbroking company. Quite apart from being a profitable part of the group, Kodde enables the company to keep abreast of developments in the port and the Rhine delta, still one of the busiest areas of coastal ship operations.

Back to ballast
Although the company never entirely forsook the ballast trade it became very much a minority cargo from the early 1980s. But what goes around, comes around and the company is now making great efforts to revolutionise the trade. One of the great problems has always been the cost of getting the commodity out of the ship followed by the last movement to the point of use. Many of the great public

works are carried out near water and some, like bridges, can actually be over water. How much better to bring the ship to the point of use and then be able to self-discharge the ballast right where it is needed? Properly organised, one direct ship load could save many lorry movements through a busy city making the whole concept not only economically sound but also environmentally friendly at the same time.

To put these ideas into practice, two ships, *Hoo Maple* and *Hoo Marlin*, were taken in hand for modification. The hatchway was divided and at the mid point a Samsung excavator was mounted. It has a sufficiently long jib to reach all parts of the hold. Beneath the excavator a garage space has been built to house a Bobcat used to facilitate the discharge and trim out the hold. It is possible to discharge a full cargo of 1,280 tonnes in less than four hours.

Although the *Hoo Maple* successfully carried and discharged the first cargo at Whitstable in January 1996, the *Hoo Marlin* provided dramatic proof of the overall concept when she brought a cargo of aggregates up the Thames for the footings of the Millennium Bridge. It was a brave venture by all concerned, carried out literally under the eyes of the City of London. The ship amply demonstrated her ability to navigate under the bridges, manoeuvre in very limited space, discharge her cargo directly to the site and sail within the six-hour tidal window. Since then a number of other cargoes, including pig iron, have been successfully carried and discharged at similar rates. To maximise the benefits and to give commercial flexibility, two more ships, *Hoo Swan* and *Hoo Dolphin*, have been similarly converted.

The future
Never a company to stand still or to rest on its laurels, there are many plans already under active consideration for the future. Some may be discarded, others may come to fruition and be successful. Some, while still involving ships, might not bear much resemblance to contemporary ideas of coastal shipping. Who can tell what the future holds but one thing is certain, the drive that built the company is still alive and well and looking energetically at the challenges of the next fifty years.

Acknowledgements
My thanks are due to the many people who helped in the compilation of this book, in particular the members of the Lapthorn family, Rachel, Tony, David and John. Others who provided invaluable assistance were: D. Beveridge, R. Bond, S. and R. Buffey, R. Childs, J. Churchward, A. Cowne, D. Dibley, J. Eltringham, R. Fenton, S. Garrett, J. Golding, D. Goubert, H. Higgs, B. Jones, J. Jordan, A. Josh, D. Montgomery, P. O'Driscoll, R. Pink, C. Reynolds, L. Spurling, J. Thompson, F. Trice, H. Williams and S. Yeates.

Apart from company sources, information has been obtained elsewhere and my sincere thanks are due to the staff of: the World Ship Society Central Record and Photograph Library, the Public Record Office, Lloyd's Register of Shipping, Bureau Veritas, the Guildhall Library, Medway Archives and the Registrar General of Shipping and Seamen.

I extend my apologies and gratitude to any person who assisted in one way or another who is not mentioned above.

Photographs have come from many sources and are acknowledged in the text.

Hoo Maple discharging aggregates at Whitstable. *[Company archives]*

FLEET LIST

Notes on the fleet list
The notation '1', '2' etc. in brackets after a ship's name indicates that she is the first, second etc. ship of that name in the fleet where the name has been used more than once regardless of whether the name comprises one or two words. The dates following the name are those of entering and leaving the company ownership or management. The histories are in chronological order according to the completion date of new ships, acquisition or taking into management. Hulls are made of steel unless otherwise stated.

On the first line is given the ship's Official Number in the British Registry followed by her tonnages, gross (g), net (n) and where known, her summer deadweight (d) at the time of acquisition. Dimensions given are the registered length x breadth x depth expressed in decimal feet for ship numbers 1 to 12, T1 to T4 and D1 and 2. The dimensions for all other ships are the overall length x breadth x summer draft expressed in metres. These dimensions are those at the time of acquisition.

On the second line are descriptions of the engine at the time of acquisition and the name of the engine builder. All are single acting oil engines and the number of cylinders is given and whether the machinery is two or four stroke i.e. 2SA or 4SA.

Changes of engine, length and tonnages are noted in chronological sequence within the histories.

The ships' histories have been corrected up to January 2001.

1. LESLIE 1947-1951
ON 104303 48g 43n 90d 76.0 x 16.0 x 4.5 feet.
26.5.1894: Completed by Smeed Dean and Co. Ltd. at Murston for Smeed Dean and Co. Ltd., Sittingbourne as the wooden spritsail barge LESLIE.
31.12.1931: Owner became the Associated Portland Cement Manufacturers Ltd., London.
30.8.1933: Sold to George Andrews and Sidney John Ellis, Sittingbourne.
16.9.1946: Sold to John Scott Hughes, London.
1.2.1947: Sold to John Henry Briant, Whitewall Shipyard, Frindsbury.
10.3.1947: Acquired by John Anthony Lapthorn, Avon Wharf, Christchurch and converted to a houseboat.
21.1.1951: Sold to Albert Felix Fewtrell, Hoo.
31.3.1953: Sold to John Maurice Gwyn, London.
1986: Sunk and abandoned at Allington.

2. ALICE MAY 1949-1966
ON 109205 89g 78n 155d 89.0 x 20.5 x 6.9 feet.
12.5.1899: Completed by W.B. MacLearon at Harwich for Robert J. Smith, Trimley, Suffolk as the wooden ketch barge ALICE MAY.
5.10.1927: Sold to R. and W. Paul Ltd., Ipswich.
25.11.1949: Acquired by John Anthony Lapthorn, Hoo.
1950: Converted to a houseboat at Hoo.
25.11.1956: Acquired by R. Lapthorn and Co. Ltd., Hoo.
1957: Re-commissioned and fitted with a 4-cyl. 4SA oil engine made by F. Perkins Ltd., Peterborough.
14.3.1966: Sold to A. Jemmett, Faversham.
10.3.1970: Sold to Mrs. V. Plummer, Camberwell. Later abandoned in the West India Dock, London and sank alongside. Lifted onto quayside in the Blackwall Basin and used by the Sea Scouts.
1982: Broken up, but register not closed until 1999.

Alice May passing Greenwich in later years. *[C.C. Beasley]*

Nellie loaded, with minimum freeboard and rolling in the wake of Queen of the Channel. [Company archives]

3. NELLIE 1951-1960
ON 114452 57g 43n 110d 79.3 x 17.8 x 5.2 feet.
19.11.1901: Completed by Charles Cremer at Faversham for himself and Benjamin Cremer as the wooden spritsail barge NELLIE.
29.6.1915: Charles Cremer, Faversham became the sole owner.
1.2.1936: Owners became Charles, Frederick and Emma Louise Cremer, Faversham.
5.7.1945: Sold to Lilias Kathleen Carden, Colchester.
1948: Sold to Daniels Brothers (Whitstable) Ltd., Whitstable.
1950: Sold to Thomas M. Glass, Point Devoran, Cornwall.
14.8.1951: Acquired by Rachel P. Lapthorn, Hoo and fitted with a 6-cyl. 4SA oil engine made by the Chrysler Corporation, Detroit, Michigan, U.S.A.
21.12.1954: Acquired by R. Lapthorn and Co. Ltd., Hoo.
11.4.1960: Sold to Geraldine M. Galton, West Hampstead.
28.10.1966: Sold to Peter M. Hicks, Brenchley.
26.2.1972: Sold to Diane Montgomery and Ann Loudoun, Sunbury.
1985: Part rebuilt as a houseboat at Twickenham.
1990: Re-engined with a 6-cyl. 4SA oil engine made by Ford Motor Co. Ltd., Dagenham.
4.1995: Sole owner became Diane Montgomery, Maldon. Further work and rigging in progress at Maldon.
Still in service 2001.

4. R.S. JACKSON 1953
ON 104324 59g 46n 77.0 x 18.1 x 5.65 feet.
23.8.1895: Completed by James Little and Charles Levy at Upnor for Julia Aldridge, Chatham and their own account as the wooden spritsail barge R.S. JACKSON.
20.10.1910: Sold to Solomon J. Brice and Walter St.J. Brice, Rochester.
15.6.1927: Sole owner became Solomon J. Brice.
26.1.1932: Tonnages became 59.10g 47.79n.
22.5.1946: Solomon J. Brice died.
2.8.1949: Joint owners became Solomon J. Brice the younger and Edith Annie Brice.
8.8.1949: Sole owner became Solomon J. Brice the younger.
6.1.1953: Acquired by Rachel P. Lapthorn, Hoo for use as a storage barge.
23.8.1953: Sank and became total loss 1.5 miles south west of Folkestone after breaking adrift from fishing vessel OCEAN VIKING while under tow from Hoo to Newhaven.

5. LANCASHIRE 1953-1955
ON 112734 53g 43n 90d 78.6 x 17.1 x 5.0 feet.
1900: Completed by Alfred White at Teynham for Eastwood and Co. Ltd., Lambeth as the wooden spritsail barge LANCASHIRE.
1943: Sold to Wakeley Brothers and Co. Ltd., Bankside.
1953: Acquired by Rachel P. Lapthorn, Hoo and fitted with a 6-cyl. 4SA oil engine made by the Chrysler Corporation, Detroit, Michigan, U.S.A.
17.4.1955: Damaged by fire at No.2 Jetty, Beckton, not repaired and used as a loading pontoon near Herring Point, Heybridge. Later buried in a landfill site near Maldon Hythe.

Lancashire. [Company archives]

6. MILDREDA 1954-1970
ON 112722 77g 51n 120d 84.8 x 19.5 x 6.3 feet.
1900: Completed by Horace Shrubsall at Ipswich for M. Mildred, Lambeth as the wooden spritsail barge MILDREDA.
1900: Sold to Wakeley Brothers and Co. Ltd., Bankside.
1919: Sold to Horace Shrubsall, East Greenwich.
1921: Sold to James D. Watson, Little Wakering, Essex.
1946: Sold to Thomas W. Schmid, Sheerness.
1950: Sold to George Andrews and Son (Freightage) Ltd., Sittingbourne.
20.3.1951: Sold to Leslie G. Strevens, Harold E. Andrews and Roydon W. Andrews, Sittingbourne and fitted with a 4-cyl. 4SA oil engine made in 1946 by the Atlantic Engine Co. Ltd.,Wishaw.
17.1.1953: Owners became H.E. Andrews and L.G. Strevens, Sittingbourne.
16.8.1954: Acquired by Rachel P. Lapthorn, Hoo and re-engined with a 6-cyl. 4SA oil engine made by the Chrysler Corporation,Detroit, Michigan, U.S.A.
21.12.1954: Acquired by R. Lapthorn and Co. Ltd., Hoo.
30.12.1956: Stranded athwart Faversham Creek with a cargo of superphosphate and declared a constructive total loss.
22.12.1970: Vessel broken up by the owner and registry closed.

Mildreda. [T. Farnham collection]

Felix and *Pride of Sheppey*. [A. Josh]

7. PRIDE OF SHEPPEY 1954-1964
ON 104946 63g 33n 120d 80.4 x 18.6 x 5.4 feet.
14.8.1900: Completed by Alfred White at Faversham for Harry Cremer, Sidney J. Chambers, Alfred Bax Chambers and Edwin Pover, Faversham as the wooden spritsail barge ETHEL.
21.11.1901: Owner became Harry Cremer, Faversham.
7.4.1902: Owners became Harry Cremer and Charles Cremer, Faversham.
14.8.1936: Owners became Charles Cremer, Emma Louise Cremer and Frederick Cremer, Faversham.
10.1.1946: Owners became Charles Cremer, Frederick Cremer and Harry Blaxland, Faversham.
1948: Sold to Thomas Schmid, Sheerness and renamed PRIDE OF SHEPPEY.
1949: Sold to George Andrews (Freightage) Ltd., Sittingbourne.
1950: Fitted with a 6-cyl. 2SA oil engine made in 1939 by Leyland Motors Ltd., Leyland.
20.2.1951: Owners became Harold E. Andrews, Leslie G. Strevens and Roydon W. Andrews, Sittingbourne.
17.1.1953: Owners became Harold E. Andrews and Leslie G. Strevens, Sittingbourne.
16.8.1954: Acquired by Rachel P. Lapthorn, Hoo.
21.12.1954: Acquired by R. Lapthorn and Co. Ltd., Hoo.
5.4.1964: Sold to West Sussex County Council, Chichester for use as an accommodation barge for a sailing school in Chichester harbour.
1972: Broken up by the owner and registry closed.

8. FELIX 1954-1972
ON 97686 79g 54n 120d 82.3 x 19.8 x 6.8 feet.
1893: Completed by J.and H. Cann at Harwich for Robert J. Smith, Walton as the wooden spritsail barge FELIX.
1928: Sold to Alfred G. Strange, Ipswich.
1931: Sold to Cranfield Brothers Ltd., Ipswich.
1954: Acquired by Rachel P. Lapthorn, Hoo and fitted with a 6-cyl. 4SA oil engine made by the Chrysler Corporation, Detroit, Michigan, U.S.A.
21.12.1954: Acquired by R. Lapthorn and Co. Ltd., Hoo.
1957: Re-engined with 6-cyl. 4SA oil engine made by F. Perkins Ltd., Peterborough.
8.5.1972: Sold to Cecil D. Richardson, Maldon.
15.11.1972: Sold to Patrick J. Law, Havant.
1.10.1976: Sold to Sarah Roberts, West Wittering.
20.8.1993: Sold to The Boat Co. Ltd., Lyne. Based in St. Katharine Dock, London and used for receptions.
1999: Sold to Robert Deards, Hoo.
Still in existence and under repair at Hoo in 2001.

9. GLADYS 1954-1956
ON 105558 80g 64n 130d 83.3 x 20.2 x 6.3 feet.
25.8.1900: Completed by W. Felton at Sandwich for Herbert Hicks, John Ayling, James Lott and Alfred Lott, Sandwich as the wooden sailing barge GLADYS.
5.10.1916: Sold to Sarah Jane Shrubsall and Gertrude Shrubsall, Blackheath.
15.6.1920: Sank in Gravesend Reach after collision with the Japanese steamer CHIFUKU MARU (5,857/1919) while on passage from London to Calais with a cargo of pitch. Raised and repaired.
29.4.1925: Sold to Horace Percy Shrubsall, East Greenwich.
28.6.1951: Sold to Ida Elizabeth Collins, London.
18.10.1954: Acquired by Donald John Carmichael, London (R. Lapthorn and Co. Ltd., Hoo, managers). Sails removed and fitted with 2 x 4-cyl. 4SA Kelvin oil engines made by the Bergius Co. Ltd.,Glasgow. Tonnages became 83g 62n.
4.5.1956: Sold to Michael Arthur Holberton Hampden-Smith, London. Re-rigged as a barge yacht.
10.7.1960: Sank near the Grain Edge Buoy after collision with the anchored Russian steamer KIROVOGRAD (2,883/1929) while on passage from London to Hoo. Wreck subsequently removed and hulked in Shepherds Creek.
10.4.1962: Registry closed.

Felix at Gravesend. *[C. Beasley]*

Gladys hulked at Shepherds Creek. *[T. Farnham collection]*

Right: Conversation piece, with *Nellie* alongside *Gladys*. [Company archives]

Below: *Mary Birch*. [Company archives]

10. MARY BIRCH 1955-1975
ON 149790 160g 114n 220d 106.0 x 21.0 x 7.4 feet.
2-cyl. 2SA oil engine made by Wm. Beardmore and Co. Ltd., Dalmuir.
1915: Completed by Wm. Beardmore and Co. Ltd., Dalmuir for the Admiralty, London as a dry cargo X lighter.
6.1920: Sold to M.S. Hilton, London.
3.1927: Sold to James Dredging, Towage and Transport Co. Ltd., London and renamed SWANAGE.
9.1935: Sold to B.W. Steamship, Tug and Lighter Co. Ltd., Hull and renamed MARY BIRCH. Re-engined with 2-cyl. 2SA oil engine made by Skandiaverken A/B., Lysekil, Sweden.
6.1954: Sold to E. Tomlinson, Hull.
8.1955: Acquired by R. Lapthorn and Co. Ltd., and S. Yeates, Hoo.
1958: Re-engined with 6-cyl. 4SA oil engine made by F. Perkins Ltd., Peterborough.
1963: Sole owner became R. Lapthorn and Co. Ltd., Hoo.
1966: Re-engined with similar machinery following a breakdown.
1975: Broken up at Queenborough.

Mavis. [Company archives]

11. MAVIS 1956-1965
ON 105088 73g 55n 120d 71.8 x 17.8 x 7.4 feet.
1896: Completed by Henry Scarr, Beverley for G. Sweeting and M. Aaron, Barton-on-Humber as the iron ketch MAVIS.
8.1922: Sold to J. Guy, Kings Lynn.
7.1927: Owners became J. Guy and E.J. Parsell, Kings Lynn. Fitted with a 4-cyl. 2SA Kelvin oil engine made by Bergius Co. Ltd., Glasgow.
4.1937: Sold to Lennard and Co. Ltd., Shoreham-by-Sea and re-engined with a 2-cyl. 2SA oil engine made by Svenskmaskinen, Sodertalje, Sweden. Sometime converted to twin screw with a 2-cyl. Ellwe and a 2-cyl. Bolinders oil engine.
11.1956: Acquired by R. Lapthorn and Co. Ltd., Hoo. Reverted to single screw and re-engined with a 6-cyl. 4SA oil engine made by F. Perkins Ltd., Peterborough.
10.1965: Sold to N.R. Stickings, Sheerness.
4.1972: Sold to M. Baker-Rogers, Port St. Mary, Isle of Man.
Thought to have been broken up in Scotland around 1973.

12. PETERNA 1958-1974
ON 149787 154g 59n 220d 105.6 x 21.0 x 7.4 feet.
2-cyl. 2SA Avance oil engine made by J.V. Svensen, Augustendal, Sweden.
1915: Completed by Short Brothers Ltd., Sunderland (Yard No. unknown but part of Contract No. 399) for the Admiralty, London as the dry cargo lighter X 73.
6.1920: Sold to M.S. Hilton, London.
3.1927: Sold to James Dredging, Towage and Transport Co. Ltd., London and renamed STUDLAND.
9.1935: Sold to B.W. Steamship, Tug and Lighter Co. Ltd., Hull and renamed HELEN BIRCH.
11.1935: Re-engined with a 2-cyl. 2SA oil engine made by Skandiaverken, Lysekil, Sweden.
1950: Sold to Peter Jepsen, Egernsund, Denmark and renamed PETERNA. Re-engined with 4-cyl. 4SA oil engine made by Alpha-Diesel A/S., Frederikshavn, Denmark.
1958: Sold to Civil and Marine Ltd., London (John Hobbins, Maldon, manager; R. Lapthorn and Co. Ltd., Hoo, technical and commercial managers).
1974: Vessel broken up by the owner and register closed.

13. YARVIC 1959-1964
ON 180249 149g 82n 193d 29.75 x 5.72 x 2.51 metres.
6-cyl. 4SA oil engine made by Crossley Brothers Ltd., Manchester.
4.1944: Completed by R. Dunstan Ltd., Thorne (Yard No. 454) for the Ministry of War Transport, London (S. Tottle, Hull, manager) as VIC 42 with original tonnages and dimensions 96g 37n 140d. 20.36 x 5.72 x 2.51 metres.
1951: Sold to Emel Transport Ltd. (N.G. Parkinson, manager), London and renamed YARVIC. Lengthened by 9.39 metres, tonnages and dimensions as on line 2.
1954: Sold to B.W. Steamship, Tug and Lighter Co. Ltd., Hull.
1959: Acquired by R. Lapthorn and Co. Ltd., Hoo.
1963: Re-engined with a 6-cyl. 4SA oil engine made by the Bergius Co. Ltd., Glasgow.
1964: Sold to East Anglian Shipping Co. Ltd., Lowestoft.
1966: Sold to Zodiac Shipping Ltd., Newry.
1968: Sold to Les Vedettes Vertes, Vannes, France and renamed TAILLEFER.
1995: Deleted from *Lloyd's Register*, continued existence doubtful.

Yarvic at Whitstable. *[Company archives]*

14. RAYCREEK 1960-1966
ON 163578 181g 91n 220d 33.27 x 6.37 x 2.28 metres.
2-cyl. 2SA oil engine made by N.V. Appingedammer Bronsmotorenfabriek, Appingedam, Netherlands.
6.1932: Completed by N.V. Scheepswerf 'Delfzijl', v/h Gebroeder Sander, Delfzijl, Netherlands (Yard No. 129) for Hendrik Ph. Bonninga, Groningen, Netherlands as KUBO.

1.1935: Sold to Samuel West Ltd., London and renamed RAYCREEK.
1940: In service with the Royal Navy as a supply vessel in Poole and London.
6.1945: Returned to pre-war owners.
1960: Acquired by R. Lapthorn and Co. Ltd., Hoo.
12.1968: Broken up by the owner at Hoo.

Raycreek. [C. Reynolds collection]

Hoocreek (1). *[C. Hill]*

15. HOOCREEK (1) 1962-1970
ON 164523 209g 100n 240d 35.82 x 6.28 x 2.48 metres.
4-cyl. 4SA oil engine made by Motorenfabrik Deutz A.G., Koln, Germany.
1928: Completed by N.V. Scheepswerf 'Gideon' v/h J. Koster Hzn., Groningen, Netherlands (Yard No. 112) for N.V. Wm. H. Muller and Co., Rotterdam, Netherlands as SEINE.
1935: Sold to Vianda Steamship Co. Ltd. (Wm. H. Muller and Co. (London) Ltd., managers), London and renamed RHONE.
1960: Sold to Mrs. Gwendoline Herbert, Bude and renamed HERB.
1961: Sold to N.W. Hardinge (Barge Owners) Ltd., London.
1962: Acquired by R. Lapthorn and Co. Ltd., Hoo and renamed HOOCREEK.
1970: Sold to David Copestake, London.
1972: Sold to P.J. Slater, Gravesend and renamed TRADE BREEZE.
1973: Sold to Eurohaven Shipping Co. Ltd., Gravesend.
1976: Sold to Stour Salvage Ltd. for demolition at The Shipyard, Mistley where work began 10.1976.

16. HOONESS 1965-1974
ON 305850 196g 120n 295d 33.38 x 6.67 x 2.53 metres.
6-cyl. 4SA oil engine made by the Bergius-Kelvin Co. Ltd., Glasgow.
1965: Completed by J.W. Cook and Co. (Wivenhoe) Ltd., Wivenhoe (Yard No. 1281) for R. Lapthorn and Co. Ltd., Hoo as HOONESS.
5.9.1974: Foundered about 35 miles north east of Barfleur in heavy weather on a voyage from London to Guernsey with a cargo of bagged cement. All the crew were saved.

Hooness. [J. Thompson]

Edward Stone at Jersey. [D. Hocquard]

17. EDWARD STONE 1965-1978
ON 308453 196g 120n 295d 33.46 x 6.68 x 2.54 metres.
6-cyl. 4SA oil engine made by the Bergius-Kelvin Co. Ltd., Glasgow.
1965: Completed by J.W. Cook and Co. (Wivenhoe) Ltd.,Wivenhoe (Yard No. 1289) for Eddystone Shipping Co. Ltd., Rochester as EDWARD STONE. Bareboat chartered to R. Lapthorn and Co. Ltd., Hoo who were also managers.
1976: Acquired by R. Lapthorn and Co. Ltd., Hoo.
1978: Sold to B.F. and R.A. Sully, T.J., A.H. and G.J. Palmer, Gravesend and renamed SUBRO VESTA.
1979: Sold to Wm. Dennison (Shapinsay) Ltd., Kirkwall and renamed HOY SOUND.
1980: Sold to B.F. and R.A. Sully, T.J., A.H. and G.J. Palmer, Gravesend and renamed SUBRO VESTA.
1985: Sold to D. and F. Investments Ltd., Grand Cayman, Cayman Islands and renamed SIMBO VESTA.
1990: Renamed SUBRO VESTA.
1990: Sold to Heriberto Munoz, San Lorenzo, Honduras and renamed SANTUARIO.
1998: Sold to S.R. Mejia Menaces, Maicao, Colombia.
Still in service 2001.

18. HOOFINCH (1) 1968-1984
ON 305755 332g 192n 463d 44.15 x 7.88 x 2.91 metres.
6-cyl. 4SA oil engine made by Blackstone and Co. Ltd., Stamford.
1964: Completed by Drypool Engineering and Dry Dock Co. Ltd., Hull (Yard No. 11) for Springwell Shipping Co. Ltd., London (Thos. E. Kettlewell and Son Ltd., Hull, managers) as SPRINGFINCH.
1968: Bareboat chartered to R. Lapthorn and Co. Ltd., Hoo and renamed HOOFINCH.
1978: Acquired by R. Lapthorn and Co. Ltd., Hoo.
1984: Sold to Medway Coasters Ltd., Rochester.
1988: Renamed COAST RUNNER.
1990: Sold to P. Beatty, Galway, Irish Republic.
13.3.1991: Damaged beyond economical repair by fire following an explosion while laid up in Galway Dock.
20.12.1993: Towed out of dock to Kinvara Quay and thence, after damaging quay wall in bad weather, to Sruthan Quay in Cashla Bay for demolition by P.O'Brien, Carraror, County Galway, Irish Republic.

Hoofinch (1) at Jersey. [D. Hocquard]

Hootact. [C. Hill]

19. HOOTACT 1970-1979
ON 337698 263g 133n 320n 41.00 x 7.07 x 2.51 metres.
4-cyl. 2SA oil engine made by N.V. Appingedammer Brons Motorenfabriek, Appingedam, Netherlands.
1950: Completed by Scheepswerf Worst en Dutmer N.V., Meppel, Netherlands (Yard No. 100) for W. Fortuin (Wijnne & Barends N.V., managers), Delfzijl, Netherlands as GESINA.
1952: Sold to Rederij 'Contact' (W. Boll, manager), Delfzijl, Netherlands and renamed CONTACT.
1970: Acquired by R. Lapthorn and Co. Ltd., Hoo and renamed HOOTACT.
1971: Re-engined with 6-cyl. 4SA oil engine made by English Electric Diesels Ltd., Kelvin Marine Division, Glasgow.
1979: Sold to B.T. Cuckow. Gillingham.
1980: Renamed CONTACT.
1981: Sold to R.G. Mullet, Gillingham.
1983: Sold to Irongable Ltd., Southampton.
1985: Sold to Caribbean Island Shipping Inc. N.V., Willemstad, Netherlands Antilles.
1989: Deleted from *Lloyd's Register*, continued existence doubtful.

20. HOOCREST (1) 1970-1980
ON 340355 490g 268n 691d 51.41 x 8.39 x 3.43 metres.
7-cyl. 4SA oil engine made by N.V. Appingedammer Brons Motorenfabriek, Appingedam, Netherlands.
1955: Completed by Gebroeder Bodewes Scheepswerf Volharding, Foxhol, Netherlands (Yard No. 134) for N.V. Vrachtvaart Maatschappij 'Ida Dekker', Rotterdam, Netherlands (E. Wagenborg's Scheepsvaart & Expedition Bedrijf N.V., Delfzijl, Netherlands, managers) as IDA-D.
1970: Acquired by R. Lapthorn and Co. Ltd., Hoo and renamed HOOCREST.
1980: Sold to Liguria Maritime Ltd., Sittingbourne.
1980: Reported sold to Mediterranean Commodities Ltd., Gibraltar and renamed ATLANTIC COMET. Laid up at Queenborough.
1984: No longer self propelled. Shortened, cut down and converted into a floating dock.
Still in existence 2001.

Hoocrest. (1). *[C. Reynolds collection]*

Hootern (1). [C. Hill]

21. HOOTERN (1)/RIVER TAW 1974-1979
ON 340504 490g 314n 711d 52.99 x 8.49 x 3.39 metres.
6-cyl. 4SA oil engine made by Klockner-Humboldt-Deutz A.G., Koln, Germany.
1957: Completed by Scheepswerf Bijlholt B.V., Foxhol, Netherlands (Yard No. 560) for Scheepvaartbedrijf Martinistad, Dordrecht, Netherlands (N.V. Scheepvaartbedrijf Gruno, Amsterdam, managers) as MARTINISTAD.
1971: Sold to West Wales Shipping Co. Ltd., Newport, Monmouthshire, and renamed DOLPHIN G.
1972: Sold to City of London Tankers Ltd., London and renamed DOLPHIN CITY.
1974: Managers became R. Lapthorn and Co. Ltd., Hoo and renamed HOOTERN.
1976: Sold to General Freight Co. Ltd., London, same managers and renamed RIVER TAW.
1979: Sold to Liguria Maritime Ltd., Sittingbourne.
1981: Sold to Ralph A. Saunders, St Kitts Nevis.
1984: Reported sunk in the Caribbean.

River Taw. [C. Hill]

Hoopride (1). *[D. Hocquard]*

22. HOOPRIDE (1) 1974-1983
ON 364606 460g 217n 580d 49.69 x 7.90 x 3.25 metres.
6-cyl. 4SA oil engine made by Maschinenbau Kiel A.G. (MaK), Kiel, Germany.
1957: Completed by Scheepswerven Gebroeder Niestern B.V., Delfzijl, Netherlands (Yard No. 249) for Rederij Gebroeder Niestern (E.Wagenborg's Scheepsvaart & Expedition Bedrijf N.V., managers), Delfzijl, Netherlands as MARTENSHOEK.
1970: Sold to Bedrijf J.B.K. Niestern (B.V. Scheepvaart D. David en Zoon, managers), Delfzijl, Netherlands and renamed BEREND N.
1970: Re-engined with 6-cyl. 4SA oil engine made in 1964 by Motorenwerke Mannheim A.G. (M.W.M.), Mannheim, Germany.
1974: Acquired by W.W. Burton Ltd., Rochester and L.J.T. Shipping Ltd., London (R. Lapthorn and Co. Ltd., Hoo, managers) and renamed HOOPRIDE.
1983: Sold to Aspenshaw Ltd., Grimsby and renamed HOOP.
1989: Sold to Ro-Farr Ship Management Ltd., Kingstown, St. Vincent and the Grenadines and renamed HELEN.
1990: Sold to K. and F. Clarkson Vasey, Kingstown, St. Vincent and the Grenadines.
1992: Sold by judicial sale to Van Brink Shipyard B.V., Rotterdam, Netherlands.
1992: Sold to Alexis Holding Ltd. (Maritime School-St.Thomas University, managers), Kingstown, St. Vincent and the Grenadines and renamed ALEXIS.
1994: Sold to Representation Ltd., Kingstown, St. Vincent and the Grenadines and renamed CHRISTOPHER 1. Tonnages (ITC'69) became 427g 209n 580d.
Still in service 2001.

23. HOOFORT (1) 1974-1982
ON 186345 446g 188n 571d 47.45 x 8.92 x 3.53 metres.
6-cyl. 2SA oil engine made by British Polar Engines Ltd., Glasgow.
1965: Completed by Ailsa Shipbuilding Co. Ltd., Troon (Yard No. 519) for the Isle of Man Steam Packet Co. Ltd., Douglas, Isle of Man as RAMSEY.
1974: Acquired by R. Lapthorn and Co. Ltd., Hoo and renamed HOOFORT.
1982: Sold to Teodore Jose Nasciamento, Cape Verde Republic and renamed BOA ENTRADA.
1987: Converted to a motor tanker.
1989: Sold to Societa Exploracion Industrie e Maritima Ltda. (SODIMAR), Cape Verde Republic and renamed ARQUIPELAGO.
Still in service 2001.

24. DELTA-G 1976-1983
ON 377064 500g 371n 798d 57.49 x 9.00 x 3.36 metres.
6-cyl. 4SA oil engine made by Motorenwerke Mannheim A.G. (M.W.M.), Mannheim,
Germany.
1958: Completed by C. Amels en Zoon Scheepswerf, Makkum, Netherlands (Yard No. 211) for D. Davids (E.Wagenborg's Scheepvaart & Expeditiebedrijf N.V., managers), Delfzijl, Netherlands as DELTA.
1963: Managers became Delta Transport Maatschappij B.V., Delfzijl, Netherlands.
1976: Acquired by Gebert Shipping Ltd., Jersey (R. Lapthorn and Co. Ltd., Hoo, managers) and renamed DELTA-G.
1983: Sold to James Shipping Co. Ltd., Jersey (Carisbrooke Shipping Ltd., Cowes, managers).
1987: Sold to Delphis Maritime Ltd., Jersey.
10.5.1987: Sank off Varberg, Sweden, in position 57.05 north, 11.55 east after taking a severe list while on passage from Landskrona to Barton on Humber with a cargo of fertilizer.

Hoofort (1). *[Fotoflite]*

Delta-G. *[C. Reynolds collection]*

Wilks. [C. Hill]

Wis. [C. Hill]

25. WILKS 1976-1985 Twin screw
ON 366101 495g 310n 1,002d 44.10 x 9.96 x 3.90 metres.
2 x 6-cyl. 4SA oil engines made by the Caterpillar Tractor Co., Peoria, Illinois, U.S.A.
1976: Completed by the Yorkshire Dry Dock Co. Ltd., Hull (Yard No. 238) for Eggar Forrester (Holdings) Ltd., London (R. Lapthorn and Co. Ltd., Hoo, managers) as WILKS.
1985: Manager became Wilks Shipping Co. Ltd., London.
1985: Owner became Wilks Shipping Co. Ltd., London (F.T. Everard and Sons Management Ltd., Greenhithe, managers).
1986: Sold to J. Harker Ltd., Hull, converted into a tanker and renamed TEESDALE H. Tonnages (ITC'69) became 499g 301n 1,050d.
1993: Owner became John H. Whitaker (Tankers) Ltd., Hull.
Still in service 2001.

26. WIS 1977-1985 Twin screw
ON 377191 491g 408n 1,036d 45.93 x 9.96 x 3.88 metres.
2 x 6-cyl. 4SA oil engines made by the Caterpillar Tractor Co., Peoria, Illinois, U.S.A.
1977: Completed by the Yorkshire Dry Dock Co. Ltd., Hull (Yard No. 241) for Eggar Forrester (Holdings) Ltd., London (R. Lapthorn and Co. Ltd., Hoo, managers) as WIS.
1985: Manager became Wilks Shipping Co. Ltd., London.
1985: Owner became Wilks Shipping Co. Ltd., London (F.T. Everard and Sons Management Ltd., Greenhithe, managers).
1986: Sold to Breydon Marine Ltd., Great Yarmouth and renamed BREYDON VENTURE.
1989: Re-engined with 2 x 6-cyl. 4SA oil engines made by A/B Volvo Penta, Gothenburg, Sweden.
1992: Managers became Genchem Marine Ltd., Ipswich.
1995: Sold to J.R. Rix and Sons Ltd., Hull, converted to a tanker and renamed RIX HAWK. Tonnages (ITC'69) became 562g 321n 1036d.
1999: Sold to the Rix Hawk Shipping Co. Ltd. (J.R. Rix and Sons Ltd., managers), Hull.
Still in service 2001.

27. ARGO-G 1978-1984
ON 377137 441g 297n 742d 50.27 x 8.89 x 2.71 metres.
8-cyl. 4SA oil engine made by Maschinenfabrik Augsburg-Nurnburg A.G. (MAN), Augsburg, Germany.
1950: Completed by Scheepswerven Gebroeder Niestern B.V., Delfzijl, Netherlands (Yard No. 241) for D. Davids (E. Wagenborg's Scheepvaart & Expeditiebedrijf N.V., managers), Delfzijl, Netherlands as ARGO.
1963: Managers became Delta Transports Maatschappij N.V., Delfzijl, Netherlands.
1972: Sold to B.V. Scheepvaart D. Davids en Zoon (B.V. Delta Transports Maatschappij, managers), Delfzijl, Netherlands and renamed ARGO D.
1974: Re-engined with 8-cyl. 4SA oil engine made in 1966 by Gebroeder Stork & Co. N.V., Hengelo, Netherlands.
1978: Acquired by Gebert Shipping Ltd., Jersey (R. Lapthorn and Co. Ltd., Hoo, managers) and renamed ARGO-G.
1983: Acquired by R. Lapthorn and Co. Ltd., Hoo and Jacobs and Tenvig (Offshore) Ltd., London (R. Lapthorn and Co. Ltd., Hoo, managers).
1984: Sold to Clive Austin, Hull.
1987: Sold to Anthony M. Sampson, Poole.
1989: Sold to Sarrka Ships Ltd., Bristol.
23.12.1989: Sustained crankshaft damage while on passage from Europoort to Gunness and towed to Rotterdam. Not repaired as owners reported bankrupt and sold to Arie Rijsdijk Boss N.V., Dordrecht, Netherlands for demolition. Re-sold to Brugse Scheepssloperij N.V., who commenced work at Bruges, Belgium during 8.1990.

Argo-G. [C. Reynolds collection]

28. WIB 1979-1985 Twin screw
ON 379856 498g 320n 1,046d 45.73 x 9.50 x 3.88 metres.
2 x 8-cyl. 4SA oil engines made by the Caterpillar Tractor Co., Peoria, Illinois, U.S.A.
1979: Completed by the Yorkshire Dry Dock Co. Ltd., Hull (Yard No. 257) for Eggar Forrester (Holdings) Ltd., London (R. Lapthorn and Co. Ltd., Hoo, managers) as WIB.
1985: Managers became Wilks Shipping Co. Ltd., London.
1985: Owner became Wilks Shipping Co. Ltd., London (F.T. Everard and Sons Management Ltd., Greenhithe, managers).
1986: Sold to Breydon Marine Ltd., Great Yarmouth and renamed BREYDON ENTERPRISE.
1992: Managers became Genchem Marine Ltd., Ipswich.
1995: Sold to T. and S. Rix Ltd. (J.R. Rix and Sons Ltd., managers), Hull. Re-engined with 2 x 8-cyl. 4SA Vee oil engines made by the Caterpillar Tractor Co., Peoria, Illinois, U.S.A., converted into a tanker and renamed RIX HARRIER. Tonnages (ITC'69) became 572g 354n 1,046d.
1999: Sold to the Rix Harrier Shipping Co. Ltd. (J.R. Rix and Sons Ltd., managers), Hull.
Still in service 2001.

29. HOOMOSS (1) 1979-1985
ON 378963 393g 266n 713d 53.04 x 8.84 x 3.25 metres.
6-cyl. 2SA oil engine made by N.V. Appingedammer Brons Motorenfabriek, Appingedam, Netherlands.
1969: Completed by N.V. Bodewes Scheepswerven, Martenshoek, Netherlands (Yard No. 504) for Rederij ms Apollo II (Beck's Scheepvaartkantoor N.V., managers), Groningen, Netherlands as APOLLO II.
1970: Renamed KOSMOS.
1979: Acquired by R. Lapthorn and Co. Ltd., Hoo and renamed HOOMOSS.

1985: Sold to Spygem Ltd. (Triton Ship Delivery, manager), London and renamed DOMBA.
1988: Sold to Tora Sea Services Ltd., Douglas, Isle of Man and renamed TORA. Registered in Kingstown, St. Vincent and the Grenadines.
1989: Re-engined with 6-cyl. 4SA oil engine made in 1973 by Mirrlees Blackstone (Stamford) Ltd., Stamford.
1994: Tonnages (ITC'69) became 478g 233n 719d.
1999: Renamed LADY GRACE.
Still in service 2001.

30. LU 1980-1985 Twin screw
ON 390744 497g 384n 1,140d 45.55 x 9.50 x 4.03 metres.
2 x 8-cyl. 4SA oil engines made by the Caterpillar Tractor Co., Peoria, Illinois, U.S.A.
1980: Completed by A/S Nordsovaerftet, Ringkoping, Denmark (Yard No. 144) for Eggar Forrester (Holdings) Ltd., London (R. Lapthorn and Co. Ltd., Hoo, managers) as LU.
1985: Managers became Wilks Shipping Co. Ltd., London.
1985: Owner became Wilks Shipping Co. Ltd., London (F.T. Everard and Sons Management Ltd., Greenhithe, managers).
1988: Sold to Atlantic Conbulk Maritime Corporation, Monrovia, Liberia, bareboat chartered to Atlanska Plovidba, Dubrovnik, Jugoslavia and renamed BOBARA.
1992: Flag state became Croatia. Tonnages (ITC'69) became 590g 350n 1,140d.
1996: Owner became Atlanska Plovidba d.d., Dubrovnik, Croatia.
Still in service (2001).

Wib. [C. Hill]

Hoomoss (1). *[D. Hocquard]*

Lu. *[C. Hill]*

31. WIGGS 1981-1985 Twin screw
ON 390745 497g 384n 1,140d 45.55 x 9.50 x 4.03 metres.
2 x 8-cyl. 4SA oil engines made by the Caterpillar Tractor Co., Peoria, Illinois, U.S.A.
1981: Completed by A/S Nordsovaerftet, Ringkoping, Denmark (Yard No. 145) for Eggar Forrester (Holdings) Ltd., London (R. Lapthorn and Co. Ltd., Hoo, managers) as WIGGS.
1985: Managers became Wilks Shipping Co. Ltd., London.
1985: Owners became Wilks Shipping Co. Ltd., London (F.T. Everard and Sons Management Ltd., Greenhithe, managers).
1988: Sold to Atlantic Conbulk Maritime Corporation, Monrovia, Liberia, bareboat chartered to Atlanska Plovidba, Dubrovnik, Jugoslavia and renamed DOLI.
1992: Flag state became Croatia. Tonnages (ITC'69) became 590g 350n 1,140d.
1996: Owner became Atlanska Plovidba d.d., Dubrovnik, Croatia.
Still in service (2001).

32. NAUTIC W 1981-1984
ON 340181 318g 177n 480d 44.89 x 8.26 x 3.11 metres.
6-cyl. 4SA oil engine made by Klockner-Humboldt-Deutz A.G., Koln, Germany.
1954: Completed by J.J. Sietas Schiffswerft, Hamburg, Germany (Yard No. 377) for J. Knuttel and H. Heinrich, Hamburg, Germany as HELGA.
1957: Managers became Robert Bornhofen K.G., Hamburg, Germany.
1961: Managers became Peter Dohle, Hamburg, Germany.
1963: Sold to Hinrich Badewien, Hamburg, Germany and renamed ERIKA B.
1976: Sold to Anglo-Norden Freight Ltd., Ipswich and renamed ANDERS W.
1980: Sold to Austrobee Ltd., Gillingham and renamed NAUTIC W. Re-engined with 6-cyl. 4SA oil engine made by Cummins Engine Co. Inc., Columbus, Indiana, U.S.A.
1981: Managers became R. Lapthorn and Co. Ltd., Hoo.
1983: Acquired by Nautic Transit, Gillingham. Same managers.
1984: Sold to J. Wiseman, Guernsey.
1985: Register transferred to Honduras.
1986: Renamed JESSICA.
1987: Renamed PRAM A.
1989: Sold to Noramco Shipping Corporation (Gulf Chartering Inc., managers, New Orleans, Louisiana, U.S.A.) and renamed NAUTIC.

1991: Sold to Net Results Ltd., Honduras and renamed MARGARET HANNAH.
7.9.1991: Reported contaminated fuel and taking water on voyage from Mobile, Alabama to St. Anna Bay, Curacao. Turned towards Jamaica but capsized after being hit by heavy wave and sank in position 16.21 north, 75.31 west. All the crew of six were saved.

33. ROVER T 1981-1983
ON 364172 418g 256n 539d 52.94 x 8.62 x 2.77 metres.
6-cyl. 4SA oil engine made by Maschinenbau Kiel A.G. (MaK), Kiel, Germany.
1962: Completed by Gebroeder Schuerenstedt K.G., Bardenfleth, Germany (Yard No. 1250) for Gerhard Ahrens, Assel, Germany as MAGULA.
1970: Sold to Johann Harms K.G., Emden, Germany and renamed BOGUMILA.
1974: Sold to Cornish Shipping Ltd., St. Austell and renamed PEROTO. Registered at Plymouth.
1978: Sold to T. and G. Shipping Ltd., Gillingham and renamed ROVER T.
1981: Managers became R. Lapthorn and Co. Ltd., Hoo.
1982: Sold to Gestor Maritime Ltd., Gillingham. Same managers.
1983: Management ceased.
20.10.1989: Demolition commenced at Bruges, Belgium by Brugse Scheepssloperij N.V.

34. SELLINA C 1982-1984
ON 398015 434g 291n 633d 48.09 x 9.17 x 3.38 metres.
6-cyl. 4SA oil engine made by VEB Schwermaschinenbau 'Karl Liebknecht' (SKL), Magdeburg, Germany.
1965: Completed by Scheepswerf 'Voorvaarts' B.V., Martenshoek, Netherlands (Yard No. 193) for Deutsche Seereederei, Rostock, Germany as SELLIN.
1981: Sold to Brian T. Cuckow, Gillingham and renamed SELLINA C. Registered in Guernsey.
1982: Managers became R. Lapthorn and Co. Ltd., Hoo.
1984: Management ceased.
1985: Sold to Patterson Shipping Ltd., Gillingham.
1989: Sold to Monica R Shipping Ltd., Valletta, Malta and renamed MONICA R. Registered at Valletta.
1990: Registered at Kingstown, St. Vincent and the Grenadines.
24.12.1991: Sank in position 55.17 north, 07.45 east after reporting that she was taking in water while on passage from Kvinesdal to Hamburg.

Nautic W. [C. Hill]

Rover T. [C. Hill]

Right: *Sellina C. [C. Hill]*

Left: *Wiggs. [C. Hill]*

35. WIRIS 1982-1985 Twin screw
ON 398974 496g 384n 1,140d 45.55 x 9.50 x 4.05 metres.
2 x 8-cyl. 4SA oil engines made by the Caterpillar Tractor Co., Peoria, Illinois, U.S.A.
1982: Completed by A/S Nordsovaerftet, Ringkoping, Denmark (Yard No. 153) for Eggar Forrester (Holdings) Ltd., London (R. Lapthorn and Co. Ltd., Hoo, managers) as WIRIS.
1985: Managers became Wilks Shipping Co. Ltd., London.
1985: Owners became Wilks Shipping Co. Ltd., London (F.T. Everard and Sons Management Ltd., Greenhithe, managers).
1988: Sold to Atlantic Conbulk Maritime Corporation, Monrovia, Liberia, bareboat chartered to Atlanska Plovidba, Dubrovnik, Jugoslavia and renamed ORASAC.
23.9.1991: Struck by artillery shells causing fire and explosions at Sibenik during Croatian hostilities. Repaired and returned to service.
1992: Flag state became Croatia. Tonnages (ITC'69) became 590g 350n 1,140d.
1996: Owner became Atlanska Plovidba d.d., Dubrovnik, Croatia.
Still in service (2001).

36. ELLEN W 1982-1984
ON 363239 428g 249n 645d 47.76 x 8.82 x 3.12 metres.
6-cyl. 4SA oil engine made by Mirrlees Blackstone (Stamford) Ltd., Stamford.
1974: Completed by Scheepswerf Bodewes B.V., Bergum, Netherlands (Yard No. 171) for Mardorf Peach and Co. Ltd., London and demise chartered to BOCM Silcocks Ltd. (Mardorf Peach and Co. Ltd., managers), London as GUY CHIPPERFIELD.
1982: Sold to W.B. Woolley (Scotland) Ltd., London (R. Lapthorn and Co. Ltd., Hoo, managers) and renamed ELLEN W.
1984: Sold to Unilever UK Central Resources Ltd., London (General Freight International Ltd., London and G.T. Gillie and Blair Ltd., Newcastle-on-Tyne, managers).
1985: Sold to Custodian Leasing Ltd., Croydon (Whitbury Shipping Ltd., Sheerness, managers).
1986: Owner became Clientcare Finance Ltd., Croydon, same managers.
1986: Owner became Clientcare Ltd., Croydon, same managers.
1993: Sold to Tara Shipping Ltd., Glenbeigh, County Kerry (Halcyon Shipping Ltd., Great Yarmouth, managers). Registered in Kingstown, St. Vincent and the Grenadines. Tonnages (ITC'69) became 459g 248n 645d.
1997: Managers became Genchem Marine Ltd., Ipswich.
Still in service (2001).

37. FREDA W. 1982-1984
ON 363247 428g 249n 645d 47.76 x 8.82 x 3.12 metres.
6-cyl. 4SA oil engine made by Mirrlees Blackstone (Stamford) Ltd., Stamford.
1974: Completed by Scheepswerf Gebroeder Coops B.V., Hoogezand, Netherlands (Yard No. 264) for Mardorf Peach and Co. Ltd., London and demise chartered to BOCM Silcocks Ltd. (Mardorf Peach and Co. Ltd., managers), London as EDWARD BROUGH.
1982: Sold to W.B. Woolley (Scotland) Ltd., London (R. Lapthorn and Co. Ltd., Hoo, managers) and renamed FREDA W.
1984: Sold to Unilever UK Central Resources Ltd., London (General Freight International Ltd., London and G.T. Gillie and Blair Ltd., Newcastle-on-Tyne, managers).
1985: Sold to Custodian Leasing Ltd., Croydon (Whitbury Shipping Ltd., Sheerness, managers).
1986: Owner became Clientcare Finance Ltd., Croydon. Same managers.
1986: Owner became Clientcare Ltd., Croydon. Same managers.
1992: Sold to Great Western Shipping Co. Ltd. (John A. Osborne, manager), Plymouth, Montserrat.
1998: Owner became John A. Osborne, Plymouth, Montserrat.
1998: Sold to Steve Ollivierre, Kingstown, St. Vincent and the Grenadines and renamed SEA SPRAY. Registered in Kingstown, St. Vincent and the Grenadines.
Still in service (2001).

Wiris. [C. Hill]

Ellen W. [C. Hill]

Freda W. [C. Hill]

Hoo Venture. [C. Hill]

38. HOO VENTURE 1982-   Twin screw
ON 389083 498g 387n 1,236d 49.99 x 9.50 x 4.05 metres.
2 x 6-cyl. 4SA oil engines made by Cummins Engine Co. Inc., Columbus, Indiana, U.S.A.
1982: Completed by the Yorkshire Dry Dock Co. Ltd., Hull (Yard No. 277) for John H. Whitaker (Holdings) Ltd., Hull and R. Lapthorn and Co. Ltd., Hoo (R. Lapthorn and Co. Ltd., Hoo, managers) as HOO VENTURE.
1994: Tonnages (ITC'69) became 671g 405n 1,230d.
1995: Acquired by R. Lapthorn and Co. Ltd., Hoo.
In present fleet (2001).

39. HOOCREEK (2) 1982-   Twin screw
ON 703258 498g 387n 1,236d 49.99 x 9.43 x 4.05 metres.
2 x 6-cyl. 4SA oil engines made by Cummins Engine Co. Inc., Columbus, Indiana, U.S.A.
1982: Completed by the Yorkshire Dry Dock Co. Ltd., Hull (Yard No. 278) for John I. Jacobs PLC, London (R. Lapthorn and Co. Ltd., Hoo, managers) as HOOCREEK. Bareboat chartered to the managers.
1989: Acquired by R. Lapthorn and Co. Ltd., Hoo.
1994: Tonnages (ITC'69) became 671g 405n 1,236d.
In present fleet (2001).

Hoocreek (2). [C. Reynolds]

Gieny S as Tower Conquest. [C. Hill]

40. GIENY S 1983-1984
ON 335910 200g 162n 430d 41.89 x 7.73 x 2.70 metres.
8-cyl 4SA Vee oil engine made by Rolls-Royce Motors Ltd., Shrewsbury.
1968: Completed by Clelands Shipbuilding Co. Ltd., Wallsend (Yard No. 303) for Tower Shipping Ltd., London as TOWER CONQUEST.
1979: Sold to Adriana B.V. (Visser & Visser Chartering B.V., managers), Rotterdam, Netherlands and renamed ELST.
1980: Sold to Siebe Elsinga, Panama and renamed GIENY S.
1983: Sold to Medway Coasters Ltd., Rochester (R. Lapthorn and Co. Ltd., managers, Hoo). Re-engined with a 6-cyl. 4SA oil engine made by Cummins Engine Co. Inc., Columbus, Indiana, U.S.A.
1984: Management ceased.
1989: Sold to J. de Roche and A. Roberts, Grenada.
1995: Used as a storage hulk at St. Georges Harbour, Grenada and later expended for use in a landfill site.

41. WHITONIA/ANTONIA B/HOOFORT (2) 1983-1994 and 1997-   Twin screw
ON 701514 498g 387n 1,234d 49.99 x 9.43 x 4.04 metres.
2 x 6-cyl. 4SA oil engines made by Cummins Charleston Inc., Charleston, South Carolina, U.S.A.
1983: Completed by the Yorkshire Dry Dock Co. Ltd., Hull (Yard No. 279) for John H. Whitaker (Tankers) Ltd., Hull (R. Lapthorn and Co. Ltd., Hoo, managers) as WHITONIA.
1984: Sold to John H. Whitaker (Holdings) Ltd., Hull. Same managers.
1993: Bareboat chartered to the managers.
1994: Bareboat chartered to Apollo Ships Ltd. (A.Whiting, manager), Rochford.
1994: Tonnages (ITC'69) became 671g 405n 1,180d.
1996: Repossessed by John H. Whitaker (Holdings) Ltd., Hull.
1997: Bareboat chartered to R. Lapthorn and Co. Ltd., Hoo and Byron Chartering and Trading Co. Ltd., Chelmsford (R. Lapthorn and Co. Ltd., Hoo, managers) and renamed ANTONIA B.
1999: Acquired by R. Lapthorn and Co. Ltd., Hoo and renamed HOOFORT.
In present fleet (2001).

Whitonia. [C. Hill]

Antonia B. [C. Reynolds]

Hoo Plover at Gravesend. [C. Reynolds]

42. HOO PLOVER 1983-   Twin screw
ON 705479 498g 387n 1,234d 49.99 x 9.50 x 4.04 metres.
2 x 6-cyl. 4SA oil engines made by Cummins Engine Co. Inc., Columbus, Indiana, U.S.A.
1983: Completed by the Yorkshire Dry Dock Co. Ltd., Hull (Yard No. 283) for John I. Jacobs PLC and Jacobs and Tenvig (Offshore) Ltd., London (R. Lapthorn and Co. Ltd., Hoo, managers) as HOO PLOVER. Bareboat chartered to the managers.
1991: Owners became John I Jacobs PLC and Jacobs Offshore Ltd., London. Same managers.
1991: Owner became John I. Jacobs PLC, London. Same managers.
1994: Tonnages (ITC'69) became 671g 405n 1,234d.
1995: Owner became Jacobs VI Ltd., London. Same managers.
1995: Owner became R. Lapthorn Shipping Ltd., Hoo. Same managers.
1996: Acquired by R. Lapthorn and Co. Ltd., Hoo.
In present fleet (2001).

Hoo Willow. [C. Reynolds]

43. HOO WILLOW 1984- Twin screw
ON 705527 498g 387n 1,234d 49.99 x 9.50 x 4.04 metres.
2 x 6-cyl. 4SA oil engines made by Cummins Engine Co. Inc., Columbus, Indiana, U.S.A.
1984: Completed by the Yorkshire Dry Dock Co. Ltd., Hull (Yard No. 285) for John I. Jacobs PLC, London (R. Lapthorn and Co. Ltd., Hoo, managers) as HOO WILLOW. Bareboat chartered to the managers.
1994: Tonnages (ITC'69) became 671g 405n 1,234d.
1995: Owner became Jacobs VI Ltd., London. Same managers.
1995: Owner became R. Lapthorn Shipping Ltd., Hoo. Same managers.
1996: Acquired by R. Lapthorn and Co. Ltd., Hoo.
In present fleet (2001).

44. HOO LAUREL 1984- Twin screw
ON 705637 794g 552n 1,394d 58.27 x 9.50 x 3.90 metres.
2 x 6-cyl. 4SA oil engines made by Cummins Engine Co. Inc., Columbus, Indiana, U.S.A.
1984: Completed by the Yorkshire Dry Dock Co. Ltd., Hull (Yard No. 286) for John I. Jacobs PLC, London (R. Lapthorn and Co. Ltd., Hoo, managers) as HOO LAUREL. Bareboat chartered to the managers.
1995: Owner became Jacobs VI Ltd., London. Same managers.
1995: Owner became R. Lapthorn Shipping Ltd., Hoo. Same managers.
1996: Acquired by R. Lapthorn and Co. Ltd., Hoo.
In present fleet (2001).

Hoo Laurel. [C. Reynolds]

Hoo Laurel [Company archives]

Hoopride (2). [C. Reynolds]

Right: *Hoopride* (2) discharging roadstone at Whitstable. *[C. Reynolds]*

Below: *Mary Coast*. *[C. Hill]*

45. HOOPRIDE (2) 1984-   Twin screw
ON 705794 794g 552n 1,394d 58.27 x 9.50 x 3.90 metres.
2 x 6-cyl. 4SA oil engines made by Cummins Engine Co. Inc., Columbus, Indiana, U.S.A.
1984: Completed by Yorkshire Dry Dock and Co. Ltd., Hull (Yard No. 287) for John I. Jacobs PLC, London (R. Lapthorn and Co. Ltd., Hoo, managers) as HOOPRIDE. Bareboat chartered to the managers.
1995: Owner became Jacobs VI Ltd., London. Same managers.
1995: Owner became R. Lapthorn Shipping Ltd., Hoo. Same managers.
1996: Acquired by R. Lapthorn and Co. Ltd., Hoo.
In present fleet (2001).

46. FINLANDIA/MARY COAST 1984-1985
ON 710009 399g 229n 515d 48.49 x 8.01 x 3.05 metres.
4-cyl. 4SA oil engine made by N.V. Appingedammer Bronsmotorenfabriek, Appingedam, Netherlands.
1961: Completed by N.V. Scheepswerf 'Appingedam', Appingedam, Netherlands (Yard No. 189) for E. Wagenborgs Scheepvaart en Expeditiebedrijf N.V., Delfzijl, Netherlands as VECHTBORG.
1972: Sold to D.P. Geuze Bedrijf N.V. (E. Wagenborg's Scheepvaart & Expeditiebedrijf N.V., managers), Delfzijl, Netherlands and renamed ESPERANCE.
1973: Sold to K.B. Bos, Delfzijl, Netherlands and renamed NOORDSTER. Same managers.
1975: Sold to Jan Stoter, Loenersloot, Netherlands, renamed FINLANDIA and registered in Panama.
1984: Sold to Harris and Dixon (Shipbrokers) Ltd., London (R. Lapthorn and Co. Ltd., Hoo, managers).
1985: Renamed MARY COAST and registered in Guernsey. Management ceased.
1986: Sold to D.J. Goubert Shipping Ltd., Guernsey.
1990: Sold to Naviera Compasion de l'Eternal S. de R.C., Delray Beach, Florida, U.S.A. and renamed COMPASION DE L'ETERNAL. Registered at San Lorenzo, Honduras.
1991: Sold to Argo Maritime Co. S.A., Belize City, Belize and renamed KEY BISCAYNE.
1993: Sold to Alavar Marine Corporation, Belize City, Belize and renamed SPLASH.
1995: Renamed KEY BISCAYNE.
1995: Sold to Inversiones Richell Inc., San Pedro Sula, Honduras and renamed RICHELL VALERIA. Tonnages (ITC'69) became 386g 245n 515d.
Still in service (2001).

Dowlais. [C. Hill]

47. DOWLAIS 1985-1995 Twin screw
ON 705844 794g 552n 1,394d 58.27 x 9.50 x 3.87 metres.
2 x 6-cyl. 4SA oil engines made by Cummins Engine Co. Inc., Columbus, Indiana, U.S.A.
1985: Completed by the Yorkshire Dry Dock Co. Ltd., Hull (Yard No. 288) for Harris and Dixon (Shipbrokers) Ltd., London (R. Lapthorn and Co. Ltd., Hoo, managers) as DOWLAIS.
1995: Sold to Franco British Chartering Ltd. and Singa Shipping Co. Ltd., London (Campbell Maritime Ltd., South Shields, managers).
Still in service (2001).

48. HOO TERN (2) 1985-   Twin screw
ON 705905 794g 552n 1,334d 58.27 x 9.50 x 3.90 metres.
2 x 6-cyl. 4SA oil engines made by Cummins Engine Co. Inc., Columbus, Indiana, U.S.A.
1985: Completed by the Yorkshire Dry Dock Co. Ltd., Hull (Yard No. 289) for John I. Jacobs PLC and Jacobs and Tenvig (Offshore) Ltd., London (R. Lapthorn and Co. Ltd., Hoo, managers) as HOO TERN. Bareboat chartered to the managers.
1991: Owners became John I. Jacobs PLC and Jacobs Offshore Ltd., London. Same managers.
1991: Owner became John I. Jacobs PLC, London. Same managers.
1995: Owner became Jacobs VI Ltd., London. Same managers.
1995: Owner became R. Lapthorn Shipping Ltd., Hoo. Same managers.
1996: Acquired by R. Lapthorn and Co. Ltd., Hoo.
In present fleet (2001).

Hoo Tern (2) *at Plymouth. [C. Reynolds]*

Upper: *Betty-Jean*. A late photograph with Lapthorn's funnel.
[*C. Reynolds*]

Lower: *Hoomoss* (2) at Marina Point. [*C. Reynolds*]

49. BETTY-JEAN/HOOMOSS (2) 1985-   Twin screw
ON 701558 794g 552n 1,360d 58.30 x 9.50 x 3.90 metres.
2 x 6-cyl. 4SA oil engines made by Cummins Engine Co. Inc., Columbus, Indiana, U.S.A.
1985: Completed by the Yorkshire Dry Dock Co. Ltd., Hull (Yard No. 291) for John H. Whitaker (Holdings) Ltd. and Bayford and Co. Ltd., Hull (R. Lapthorn and Co. Ltd., Hoo, managers) as BETTY-JEAN.
1995: Bareboat chartered to R. Lapthorn and Co. Ltd., Hoo and Byron Chartering and Trading Co. Ltd., Chelmsford. Same managers.
1999: Acquired by R. Lapthorn and Co. Ltd., Hoo and renamed HOOMOSS.
In present fleet (2001).

Hoo Swan. [C. Reynolds]

Hoo Marlin at Dordrecht. [C. Reynolds]

50. HOO SWAN 1986-   Twin screw
ON 709744 794g 552n 1,412d 58.30 x 9.50 x 3.90 metres.
2 x 6-cyl. 4SA oil engines made by Cummins Engine Co. Inc., Columbus, Indiana, U.S.A.
1986: Completed by the Yorkshire Dry Dock Co. Ltd., Hull (Yard No. 292) for Jacobs and Tenvig (Offshore) Ltd., London and R. Lapthorn and Co. Ltd., Hoo (R. Lapthorn and Co. Ltd., Hoo, managers) as HOO SWAN. Bareboat chartered to R. Lapthorn (Holdings) Ltd., Hoo.
1989: Owners became Jacobs and Tenvig (Offshore) Ltd., London and R. Lapthorn and Co. Ltd., Hoo. Same managers.
1991: Owners became John I. Jacobs PLC, London and R. Lapthorn and Co. Ltd., Hoo. Same managers.
1995: Owners became Jacobs VI Ltd., London and R. Lapthorn and Co. Ltd., Hoo. Same managers.
1995: Owners became R. Lapthorn Shipping Ltd. and R. Lapthorn and Co. Ltd., Hoo. Same managers.
1996: Acquired by R. Lapthorn and Co. Ltd., Hoo.

2000: Converted for self discharge.
In present fleet (2001).

51. HOO MARLIN 1986-   Twin screw
ON 709792 794g 552n 1,412d 58.30 x 9.50 x 3.90 metres.
2 x 6-cyl. 4SA oil engines made by Cummins Charleston Inc., Charleston, South Carolina, U.S.A.
1986: Completed by the Yorkshire Dry Dock Co. Ltd., Hull (Yard No. 293) for Jacobs and Partners Ltd., London (R. Lapthorn and Co. Ltd., Hoo, managers) as HOO MARLIN. Bareboat chartered to the managers.
1995: Owner became Jacobs VI Ltd., London. Same managers.
1995: Owner became R. Lapthorn Shipping Ltd., Hoo. Same managers.
1996: Acquired by R. Lapthorn and Co. Ltd., Hoo.
1997: Converted for self discharge.
In present fleet (2001).

Hoo Marlin converted. *[C. Reynolds]*

52. HOO DOLPHIN 1986-   Twin screw
ON 709866 794g 552n 1,412d 58.27 x 9.55 x 3.90 metres.
2 x 6-cyl. 4SA oil engines made by Cummins Charleston Inc., Charleston, South Carolina, U.S.A.
1986: Completed by the Yorkshire Dry Dock Co. Ltd., Hull (Yard No. 294) for Jacobs and Partners Ltd., London (R. Lapthorn and Co. Ltd., Hoo, managers) as HOO DOLPHIN. Bareboat chartered to the managers.
1995: Owner became Jacobs VI Ltd., London. Same managers.
1995: Owner became R. Lapthorn Shipping Ltd., Hoo. Same managers.
1996: Acquired by R. Lapthorn and Co. Ltd., Hoo.
2000: Converted for self discharge.
In present fleet (2001).

Hoo Dolphin. [C. Hill]

53. HOOCREST (2) 1986-   Twin screw
ON 709945 794g 552n 1,400d 58.30 x 9.56 x 3.90 metres.
2 x 6-cyl. 4SA oil engines made by Cummins Engine Co. Inc., Columbus, Indiana, U.S.A.
1986: Completed by the Yorkshire Dry Dock Co. Ltd., Hull (Yard No. 295) for John I. Jacobs PLC, London (R. Lapthorn and Co. Ltd., Hoo, managers) as HOOCREST. Bareboat chartered to the managers.
1995: Owner became Jacobs VI Ltd., London. Same managers.
1995: Owner became R. Lapthorn Shipping Ltd., Hoo. Same managers.
1996: Acquired by R. Lapthorn and Co. Ltd., Hoo.
In present fleet (2001).

54. HOO FINCH (2) 1988-   Twin screw
ON 717023 794g 552n 1,377d 58.27 x 9.50 x 3.90 metres.
2 x 6-cyl. 4SA oil engines made by Cummins Engine Co. Inc., Columbus, Indiana, U.S.A.
1988: Completed by the Yorkshire Dry Dock Co. Ltd., Hull (Yard No. 316) for Jacobs and Partners Ltd., London and R. Lapthorn and Co. Ltd., Hoo (R. Lapthorn and Co. Ltd., Hoo, managers) as HOO FINCH. Bareboat chartered to R. Lapthorn (Holdings) Ltd., Hoo.
1995: Owners became Jacobs VI Ltd., London and R. Lapthorn and Co. Ltd., Hoo. Same managers.
1995: Owners became R. Lapthorn Shipping Ltd., and R. Lapthorn and Co. Ltd.,Hoo. Same managers.
1996: Acquired by R. Lapthorn and Co. Ltd., Hoo.
In present fleet (2001).

Above: *Hoocrest* (2). *[C. Reynolds]*

Below: *Hoo Finch* (2). *[Fotoflite]*

Hoo Robin. [Fotoflite]

Hoo Robin in calmer waters at Holtenau. *[C. Reynolds]*

55. HOO ROBIN 1989-   Twin screw
ON 717095 794g 552n 1,377d 58.27 x 9.50 x 3.90 metres.
2 x 6-cyl. 4SA oil engines made by Cummins Engine Co. Inc., Columbus, Indiana, U.S.A.
1989: Completed by the Yorkshire Dry Dock Co. Ltd., Hull (Yard No. 317) for Jacobs and Partners Ltd., London (R. Lapthorn and Co. Ltd., Hoo, managers) as HOO ROBIN. Bareboat chartered to the managers.
1995: Owner became Jacobs VI Ltd., London. Same managers.
1995: Owner became R. Lapthorn Shipping Ltd., Hoo. Same managers.
1996: Acquired by R. Lapthorn and Co. Ltd., Hoo.
In present fleet (2001).

Hoo Swift. [C. Reynolds]

56. HOO SWIFT 1989- Twin screw
ON 717199 794g 552n 1,377d 58.27 x 9.49 x 3.90 metres.
2 x 6-cyl. 4SA oil engines made by Cummins Engine Co. Inc., Columbus, Indiana, U.S.A.
1989: Completed by the Yorkshire Dry Dock Co. Ltd., Hull (Yard No. 318) for Jacobs and Partners Ltd., London and R. Lapthorn and Co. Ltd., Hoo (R. Lapthorn and Co. Ltd., Hoo, managers) as HOO SWIFT. Bareboat chartered to R. Lapthorn (Holdings) Ltd., Hoo.
1995: Owners became Jacobs VI Ltd., London and R. Lapthorn and Co. Ltd., Hoo. Same managers.
1995: Owners became R. Lapthorn Shipping Ltd., and R. Lapthorn and Co. Ltd., Hoo. Same managers.
1996: Acquired by R. Lapthorn and Co. Ltd., Hoo.
In present fleet (2001).

Hoo Swift preparing to load at Europoort. Note the bow star motif. [C. Reynolds]

Hoo Maple at Port Barrier. [C. Reynolds]

57. HOO MAPLE 1989-   Twin screw
ON 717342 794g 552n 1,400d 58.30 x 9.49 x 3.90 metres.
2 x 6-cyl. 4SA oil engines made by Cummins Charleston Inc., Charleston, South Carolina, U.S.A.
1989: Completed by the Yorkshire Dry Dock Co. Ltd., Hull (Yard No. 319) for Jacobs and Partners Ltd., London (R. Lapthorn and Co. Ltd., Hoo, managers) as HOO MAPLE. Bareboat chartered to the managers.
1995: Owner became Jacobs VI Ltd., London. Same managers.
1995: Owner became R. Lapthorn Shipping Ltd., Hoo. Same managers.
1995: Converted for self discharge.
1996: Acquired by R. Lapthorn and Co. Ltd., Hoo.
In present fleet (2001).

58. HOO BEECH 1989-   Twin screw
ON 717404 794g 552n 1,399d 58.30 x 9.49 x 3.90 metres.
2 x 6-cyl. 4SA oil engine made by Cummins Engine Co. Inc., Columbus, Indiana, U.S.A.
1989: Completed by the Yorkshire Dry Dock Co. Ltd., Hull (Yard No. 320) for Jacobs and Partners Ltd., London (R. Lapthorn and Co. Ltd., Hoo, managers) as HOO BEECH. Bareboat chartered to the managers.
1995: Owner became Jacobs VI Ltd., London. Same managers.
1995: Owner became R. Lapthorn Shipping Ltd., Hoo. Same managers.
1996: Acquired by R. Lapthorn and Co. Ltd., Hoo.
In present fleet (2001).

Hoo Beech. [C. Reynolds]

Ilona G. [Fotoflite]

59. ILONA G. 1990-
ON 718946   999g 575n 1,700d   69.10 x 10.76 x 3.86 metres.
12-cyl. 4SA Vee oil engine made by Cummins Engine Co. Ltd., Daventry.
1990: Completed by the Yorkshire Dry Dock Co. Ltd., Hull (Yard No. 323) for Harris and Dixon (Shipbrokers) Ltd., London (R. Lapthorn and Co. Ltd., Hoo, managers) as ILONA G.
1996: Bareboat chartered to R. Lapthorn and Co. Ltd., Hoo and Byron Chartering and Trading Co. Ltd., Chelmsford (R. Lapthorn and Co. Ltd., Hoo, managers).
1999: R. Lapthorn and Co. Ltd., Hoo became sole bareboat charterers.
In present fleet (2001).

60. ANNA MARIA/ANNA MERYL 1991 and 1994-
ON 709211   999g 565n 1,700d   69.10 x 10.76 x 3.85 metres.
12-cyl. 4SA Vee oil engine made by Cummins Engine Co. Ltd., Daventry.
1991: Completed by the Yorkshire Dry Dock Co. Ltd., Hull (Yard No. 324) for Beulah Shipping Ltd., Nicosia, Cyprus (R. Lapthorn and Co. Ltd., Hoo, managers) as ANNA MARIA. Registered in Limassol, Cyprus.
1991: Managers became Capelle Chartering and Trading B.V., Rotterdam, Netherlands.
1994: Acquired by R. Lapthorn and Co. Ltd., Hoo and renamed ANNA MERYL. Registered in the United Kingdom and Official Number became 725514. Bareboat chartered to Byron Chartering and Trading Co. Ltd., Chelmsford (R. Lapthorn and Co. Ltd., Hoo, managers).
1999: Bareboat charter terminated.
In present fleet (2001).

Anna Maria. [C. Hill]

Above: *Anna Meryl*. [C. Reynolds]

Below: *Hoo Falcon*. [Company archives]

61. HOO FALCON 1991- Twin screw
ON 721913   1,382g 794n 2,225d   77.80 x 11.10 x 4.02 metres.
2 x 6-cyl. 4SA oil engines made by Cummins Charleston Inc., Charleston, South Carolina, U.S.A.
1991: Completed by the Yorkshire Dry Dock Co. Ltd., Hull (Yard No. 325) for John I. Jacobs PLC, London and R. Lapthorn and Co. Ltd., Hoo (R. Lapthorn and Co. Ltd., Hoo, managers) as HOO FALCON. Bareboat chartered to R. Lapthorn (Holdings) Ltd., Hoo.
1995: Owners became Jacobs VI Ltd., London and R. Lapthorn and Co. Ltd., Hoo. Same managers.
1995: Owners became R. Lapthorn Shipping Ltd., and R. Lapthorn and Co. Ltd., Hoo.
1996: Acquired by R. Lapthorn and Co. Ltd., Hoo.
In present fleet (2001).

Bowcliffe. [C. Reynolds]

62. BOWCLIFFE/FAST KEN 1992- Twin screw
ON 720331 1,382g 794n 2,220d 77.80 x 11.10 x 4.03 metres.
2 x 6-cyl. 4SA oil engines made by Cummins Engine Co. Inc., Columbus, Indiana, U.S.A.
1992: Completed by the Yorkshire Dry Dock Co. Ltd., Hull (Yard No. 326) for John H. Whitaker (Holdings) Ltd., Hull and Bayford and Co. Ltd. Leeds (R. Lapthorn and Co. Ltd., Hoo, managers) as BOWCLIFFE.
1994: Time chartered to Fastlines Belgium N.V., Antwerp, Belgium and renamed FAST KEN. Same managers.
1999: Time charter completed and renamed BOWCLIFFE. Same managers.
In present fleet (2001).

Fast Ken. [C. Reynolds]

74

Hoo Larch in Antwerp. *[C. Reynolds]*

63. HOO LARCH 1992-   Twin screw
ON 722169   1,382g 794n 2,225d   77.80 x 11.10 x 4.02 metres.
2 x 6-cyl. 4SA oil engines made by Cummins Engine Co. Ltd., Daventry.
1992: Completed by the Yorkshire Dry Dock Co. Ltd., Hull (Yard No. 327) for John I. Jacobs PLC, London (R. Lapthorn and Co. Ltd., Hoo, managers) as HOO LARCH. Bareboat chartered to the managers.
1995: Owner became Jacobs VI Ltd., London. Same managers.
1995: Owner became R. Lapthorn Shipping Ltd., Hoo. Same managers.
1996: Acquired by R. Lapthorn and Co. Ltd., Hoo.
In present fleet (2001).

64. HOO KESTREL 1993-   Twin screw
ON 722234   1,382g 794n 2,225d   77.80 x 11.10 x 3.95 metres.
2 x 6-cyl. 4SA oil engines made by Cummins Engine Co. Inc., Columbus, Indiana, U.S.A.
1993: Completed by the Yorkshire Dry Dock Co. Ltd., Hull (Yard No. 328) for Jacobs and Partners Ltd., London and R. Lapthorn and Co. Ltd., Hoo (R. Lapthorn and Co. Ltd., Hoo, managers) as HOO KESTREL. Bareboat chartered to R. Lapthorn (Holdings) Ltd., Hoo.
1995: Owners became Jacobs VI Ltd., London and R. Lapthorn and Co. Ltd., Hoo. Same managers.
1995: Owners became R. Lapthorn Shipping Ltd., Hoo and R. Lapthorn and Co. Ltd., Hoo. Same managers.
1996: Acquired by R. Lapthorn and Co. Ltd., Hoo.
In present fleet (2001).

Hoo Kestrel. [Fotoflite]

Nicky L. [C. Reynolds]

65. NICKY L 1998-1999
ON 712664 ,1,220g 729n 1,897d 78.44 x 10.80 x 4.12 metres.
16-cyl. 4SA Vee oil engine made by the Caterpillar Tractor Co., Peoria, Illinois, U.S.A.
1976: Completed by Scheepswerf en Machinefabriek Barkmeijer Stroobos B.V., Stroobos, Netherlands (Yard No. 204) for H. en P. Holwerda (Scheepvaartkantoor Holwerda, managers), Heerenveen, Netherlands as ROELOF HOLWERDA. (Tonnages: 938g 600n 1,599d. Dimensions 65.82 x 10.80 x 4.29 metres).
1981: Owner became Rederij Roelof Holwerda (Holwerda Scheepvaart B.V., managers), Heerenveen, Netherlands and renamed TANJA HOLWERDA.
1986: Owner became Rederij H. en P. Holwerda, Heerenveen, Netherlands.
1987: Owner became Holwerda Scheepvaart B.V., Limassol, Cyprus and renamed THE DUTCH.
27.7.1987: Took heavy list 70 miles east of Bridlington in position 54.33 north, 01.25 east on voyage from Archangel to Boston with timber. Towed into Hull, declared a constructive total loss and *15.9.1987* handed to salvors.
1987: Sold to the Magrix Shipping Co. Ltd. (J.R. Rix and Sons *Ltd., managers), Hull and renamed MAGRIX. Lengthened to 78.44 metres, tonnages becoming 998g 699n 1,898d.
1994: Tonnages (ITC'69) became 1,220g 729n 1,897d.
2.3.1998: F.T. Everard and Sons Management Ltd., Greenhithe became chartering managers.
1998: Sold to Waveney Shipping 2 PLC, Lowestoft (R. Lapthorn and Co. Ltd., Hoo, managers) and renamed NICKY L. Time chartered to managers.
1999: Sold to Abalone Shipping Services S.A., Panama (Mainport Marine Services, Schiedam, Netherlands, managers) and renamed ABALONE. Registered in Belize. Still in service (2001).

Tugs and service craft

T1. SALLY 1952-1969
Former fishing boat. Registered at Faversham as F96.
56 HP Perkins engine.
1952 Acquired.
1969: Sold to Peter Woodger, Merstham.
1973: Sold to unknown buyer at Queenborough.
Fate unknown.

T2. HOORAY 1954-1969
Former ship's lifeboat converted at Colchester.
56 HP Perkins engine.
1954: Acquired and named HOORAY.
1969: Sold to Fred. Trice, Gillingham and renamed FREEBOY.
1983: Sold to unknown buyer at Erith.
1993: Sold to unknown buyer in Medway area.
Fate unknown.

Sally. [Company archives]

Hooray. [Company archives]

Hooligan. [Company archives]

T3. HOOLIGAN 1961-1974) Tug.
ON 305511 32g 56.0 x 12.6 x 5.1 feet.
3-cyl. 2SA oil engine made by H. Widdop and Co. Ltd., Keighley.
1932: Completed by the Rowhedge Iron Works Co. Ltd., Rowhedge for the War Department, London as CRYSTAL II.
8.1956: Sold to R.L. Baker, Canvey Island.
1961: Acquired by R. Lapthorn and Co. Ltd., Hoo and renamed HOOLIGAN. Re-engined with a 4-cyl. 4SA oil engine made by F. Perkins Ltd., Peterborough.
1967: Re-engined with a similar Perkins engine after breakdown.
1974: Sold to the Acorn Shipyard Ltd., Rochester and renamed ACORN.
1990: Broken up by the owner at Rochester.

T4. HOODWINK
Launch/tug.

Motor barges managed in the explosives trade for Darling Brothers Ltd.

D1. REVIVAL 1957-1978)
ON 109210 73g 54n 84.0 x 20.2 x 5.6 feet.
19.7.1901: Completed by William Orvis and Co., Ipswich for Eldred Watkins, Stoke, Ipswich as the wooden spritsail barge ELDRED WATKINS.
25.2.1934: Sunk in the River Orwell at Buttermans Bay buoys after being struck by the British steamer SHEAF GARTH (1,927/1921) whilst loading maize alongside the Greek steamer K. KTISTAKIS (4,291/1907). Subsequently raised.
4.1.1935: Sold to F.W. Horlock, Mistley, repaired and renamed REVIVAL.
19.10.1938: Sold to Marcus F. Horlock and Walter R. Smith, Mistley.
31.10.1938: Sold to M.F. Horlock and Co. Ltd., Mistley.
18.11.1938: Sold to Successors to Thomas F. Wood (Gravesend) Ltd., Gravesend.
21.4.1953: Sold to Imperial Chemical Industries Ltd., London.
23.8.1957: Acquired by Darling Brothers Ltd., London.
21.11.1957: Sails removed and fitted with a 4-cyl. 4SA oil engine made by F. Perkins Ltd., Peterborough.
8.1967: Re-engined with a similar engine following breakdown.
8.2.1978: Sold to Graham Reeve, Dolphin Sailing Barge Museum, Sittingbourne and re-rigged at the Dolphin Yard, Sittingbourne.
25.6.1982: Sold to Le Youdec, France.

Felix and Revival. [A. Josh]

D2. WATER LILY 1957-1978
ON 114334 75g 58n 83.0 x 21.0 x 6.1 feet.
18.6.1902: Completed by Gill and Son Ltd., Rochester for James Spitty, Bradwell-on-Sea as the wooden spritsail barge WATER LILY.
29.12.1911: Owner became John Spitty, Bradwell-on-Sea.
10.9.1912: Sold to Clement Wright Parker, Bradwell-on-Sea.
5.7.1932: Sold to Wakeley Brothers and Co. Ltd., Bankside, London.
8.11.1948: Acquired by Darling Brothers Ltd., London. Fitted with 3-cyl 4SA Kelvin oil engine made by the Bergius Co. Ltd., Glasgow.
18.3.1978: Sold to Gethyn Charles Swan, Wrentham for use as a houseboat.
1986: Hulked at Pin Mill, River Orwell.

Water Lily. [T. Farnham collection]

R. Lapthorn & Co. Ltd.

R. Lapthorn & Co. Ltd. and
John H. Whitaker (Holdings) Ltd.

Beulah Shipping Ltd.

Harris & Dixon (Shipbrokers) Ltd.

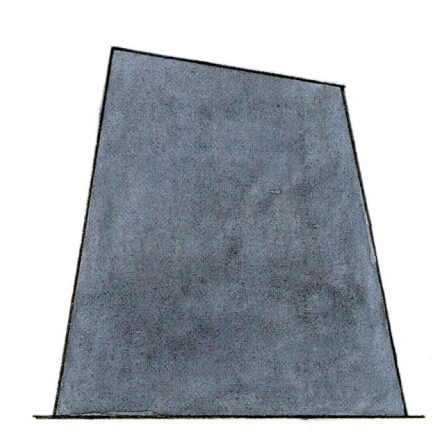

Waveney Shipping 2plc.

(Early)   John H. Whitaker (Holdings) Ltd and Bayford & Co. Ltd.   (Later)

John H. Whitaker (Holdings) Ltd.

Eggar Forrester (Holdings) Ltd.

General Freight Co. Ltd.

Gebert Shipping Ltd.

FLEET PROGRAMME.

The table sets out the loading and discharging ports together with the current and projected cargoes for the fleet during a representative period in mid-March 2001.

Vessel	Voyage no.	Loaded	Discharged	Port	Cargo.
ANNA MERYL	003.	14.3.01.	16.3.01.	Kings Lynn. Rotterdam.	Wheat.
	004.			Rotterdam. Kings Lynn.	Meal.
	005.			Rotterdam. Kings Lynn.	Meal.
HOO BEECH	003.	14.3.01	16.3.01.	Dean Quarry. Briton Ferry.	Stone.
	004.			Swansea. Ostend.	Coal.
	005.			Amsterdam. Wisbech.	Steel.
BOWCLIFFE	003.	14.3.01.	20.3.01.	Ghent. Tower Wharf.	Steel.
	004.			Ghent. Tower Wharf.	Steel.
	005.			Ghent. Sutton Bridge.	Steel.

Hoo Beech. [Fotoflite]

HOOCREEK	Repairs at Ipswich.				
	002			Rotterdam.	Pellets.
				Plymouth.	
	003.			Dean Quarry.	Stone.
				Dagenham.	
HOOCREST	003.	14.3.01.		Calais.	Stone.
			16.3.01.	Granite Wharf.	
	004.			Rotterdam.	Anthracite.
				Perth.	
	005.			Berwick.	Stone.
				Terneuzen.	
HOO DOLPHIN	003.	14.3.01.		Par.	Stone.
			16.3.01.	Erith.	
	004.			Denton.	Lead dross.
				Hoboken.	
	005.			Flushing.	Furnace ash.
				Ipswich.	
HOO FALCON	003.	14.3.01.		Kings Lynn.	Wheat.
			19.3.01.	Amsterdam.	
	004.			Terneuzen.	Fertilizer.
				Silloth.	
	005.			Dean Quarry.	Stone.
				Ipswich.	

Hoo Falcon. [C. Reynolds]

HOO FINCH	003.	14.3.01.		Rotterdam.	Soya meal
			15.3.01.	New Holland.	
	004.			Kings Lynn.	Barley.
				Ruisbroek.	
	005.			Antwerp.	Fertilizer.
				Gunness.	
HOOFORT	003.	13.3.01.		Immingham.	Petroleum coke.
			15.3.01.	Rotterdam.	
	004			Amsterdam.	Fertilizer.
				Kings Lynn.	
	005.			Kings Lynn.	Malting barley.
				Bremen.	
ILONA G	003.	13.3.01.		Sutton Bridge.	Wheat.
			15.3.01.	Rotterdam.	
	004.			Europoort.	Meal.
				Boston.	
	005.			Sutton Bridge.	Wheat.
				Amsterdam.	

Top: *Hoo Finch* (2). *[C. Reynolds]*

Right: *Ilona G* loading coal at Europoort. *[C. Reynolds]*

Hoo Kestrel discharging at Leixoes. *[C. Reynolds]*

HOO KESTREL	002.	14.3.01.	19.3.01.	Ghent. Sutton Bridge.	Steel
	003.			Ghent. Boston.	Steel.
	004.			Lowestoft. Ruisbroek.	Barley.
HOO LAUREL	003.	14.3.01.	19.3.01.	Rotterdam. Honfleur.	Magnesite.
	004.			Southampton. Rotterdam.	Barley.
	005.			Ghent. Sutton Bridge.	Steel.
HOO LARCH	002.	14.3.01.	19.3.01.	Southampton. Zwijndrecht.	Wheat.
	003.			Ghent. Sutton Bridge.	Steel.
	004.			Rotterdam. Gunness.	Magnesite.
HOO MARLIN	004.	12.3.01.	15.3.01.	Port Barrier. Rochester.	Stone.
	005.			Ipswich. Murphy's Wharf.	Sand.
	006.			Calais. Mulberry Wharf.	Stone.
HOOMOSS	004.	13.3.01.	16.3.01.	Le Legue. Vlaardingen.	Clay.
	005.			Rotterdam. Dunball.	Anthracite.
	006.			Fowey. Rotterdam.	Clay.

HOO MAPLE	003.	13.3.01.		Dean Quarry.	Stone.
			14.3.01	Rye.	
	004.			Calais.	Stone.
				Ramsgate.	
	005.			Calais.	Stone.
				Mulberry Wharf.	
HOO PLOVER	003.	10.3.01.		Hamburg.	Potash.
			14.3.01.	Montrose.	
	004			Sutton Bridge.	Wheat.
				Rotterdam.	
	005.			Rotterdam.	Meal.
				Southampton.	
HOOPRIDE	Special Survey.				
	002.			Bremen.	Fertilizers.
				Gunness.	
	003.			Boston.	Barley.
				Bremen.	
HOO ROBIN	003.	14.3.01.		Kings Lynn.	Wheat.
			16.3.01.	Ruisbroek.	
	004.			Antwerp.	Bauxite.
				Killingholme.	
	005.			Kings Lynn.	Wheat.
				Rotterdam.	
HOO SWIFT	003.	14.3.01.		Teignmouth.	Clay.
			17.3.01.	Rotterdam.	
	004.			Amsterdam.	Furnace ash.
				Gunness.	
	005.			Boston.	Barley.
				Walsoorden.	

Hoo Plover arriving at Whitstable. *[C. Reynolds]*

Hoo Swan. [C. Reynolds]

HOO SWAN	004.	14.3.01.	15.3.01.	Calais. Littlehampton.	Stone.
	005.			Calais. Mulberry Wharf.	Stone.
	006.			Calais. Mulberry Wharf.	Stone.
HOO TERN	002.	13.3.01.	15.3.01.	Kings Lynn. Rotterdam.	Wheat.
	003.			Antwerp. Plymouth.	Ammonium nitrate.
	004.			Southampton. Rotterdam.	Barley.
HOO VENTURE	004.	14.3.01.	16.3.01.	Rotterdam. Killingholme.	Vermiculite.
	005.			Rotterdam. Southampton.	Wheat.
	006.			Port Barrier. Dagenham.	Stone.
HOO WILLOW	002.	14.3.01.	19.3.01.	Dean Quarry. Ipswich.	Stone.
	003.			Terneuzen. Poole.	Fertilizers.
	004.			Dean Quarry. Rye.	Stone.

INDEX OF SHIPS

Index to ships owned or managed by R. Lapthorn and Co. Ltd showing the fleet numbers and pages where there is a reference to or a picture of the ship. The names in capitals are those carried whilst in company ownership or management. The notation (1) or (2) after the name in the list indicates that the ship was the first or second of that name in the fleet.

Name	Ship No.	Page
Abalone	65	76
Acorn	T3	21,78
Alexis	22	48
ALICE MAY	2	8,10,16,27,36
Anders W	32	54
ANNA MARIA	60	32,72
ANNA MERYL	60	6,32,72,73,81
ANTONIA B	41	28,59,60
Apollo II	29	52
Argo	27	51
Argo D	27	51
ARGO-G	27	25,51
Arquipelago	23	48
Atlantic Comet	20	22,46
Berend N	22	24,48
BETTY-JEAN	49	28,65
Boa Entrada	23	48
Bobara	30	52
Bogumila	33	54
BOWCLIFFE	62	28,29,74,81
Breydon Enterprise	28	52
Breydon Venture	26	51
Christopher 1	22	48
Crystal II	T3	10,78
Coast Runner	18	45
Compasion de l'Eternal	46	63
Contact	19	46
Delta	24	48
DELTA-G	24	25,48,49
Doli	31	54
Dolphin City	21	23,47
Dolphin G	21	47
Domba	29	52
DOWLAIS	47	33,64
Edward Brough	37	56
EDWARD STONE	17	15,45
Eldred Watkins	D1	79
ELLEN W	36	33,56,57
Elst	40	59
Erika B	32	54
Esperance	46	63
Ethel	7	39
FAST KEN	62	28,74
FELIX	8	9-11,39,40,79
FINLANDIA	46	33,63
FREDA W	37	33,56,57
Gesina	19	46
GIENY S	40	33,59
GLADYS	9	10,23,39-41
Guy Chipperfield	36	56
Helen	22	48
Helen Birch	12	42
Helga	32	54
Herb	15	17,44
HOO BEECH	58	31,71,81
HOOCREEK (1)	15	17,21,44
HOOCREEK (2)	39	29,30,58,82
HOOCREST (1)	20	19,22-4,46
HOOCREST (2)	53	68,88
HOO DOLPHIN	52	30,35,67,82
HOODWINK	T4	11,78
HOO FALCON	61	30,73,82
HOOFINCH (1)	18	22,45
HOO FINCH (2)	54	30,31,68,83
HOOFORT (1)	23	22,24,48,49
HOOFORT (2)	41	28,59,83
HOO KESTREL	64	30,32,33,75,84
HOO LARCH	63	75,84
HOO LAUREL	44	29,61,62,84
HOOLIGAN	T3	10,11,21,78
HOO MAPLE	57	31,35,71,85
HOO MARLIN	51	34,35,66,67,84
HOOMOSS (1)	29	22,23,52,53
HOOMOSS (2)	49	28,65,84
HOONESS	16	15,44
Hoop	22	48
HOO PLOVER	42	29,60,85
HOOPRIDE (1)	22	18,19,21-2, 24,48
HOOPRIDE (2)	45	62,63,85
HOORAY	T2	10,14,22,77
HOO ROBIN	55	30,69,85
HOO SWAN	50	29,30,35,66,86
HOO SWIFT	56	30,70,85
HOOTACT	19	19,22,24,46
HOOTERN (1)	21	22,23,47
HOO TERN (2)	48	64, 86
HOO VENTURE	38	28,30-3,58,86
HOO WILLOW	43	29,61,86
Hoy Sound	17	45
Ida-D	20	46
ILONA-G	59	31,32,72,83
Jessica	32	54
Key Biscayne	46	63
Kosmos	29	52
Kubo	14	43
Lady Grace	29	52
LANCASHIRE	5	9,37,38
LESLIE	1	7,27,36
LU	30	52,53
Magrix	65	76
Magula	33	54
Margaret Hannah	32	54
Martinistad	21	47
Martenshoek	22	48
MARY BIRCH	10	11-13,15,16,18,41
MARY COAST	46	33,63
MAVIS	11	12,13,42
MILDREDA	6	9,38
Monica R	34	54
Nautic	32	54
NAUTIC W	32	33,54,55
NELLIE	3	4,8,10,11,37,41
NICKY L	65	33,76
Noordster	46	63
Orasac	35	56
Peroto	33	54
PETERNA	12	12,23,42
Pram A	32	54
PRIDE OF SHEPPEY	7	9,39
R.S. JACKSON	4	10,37
Ramsey	23	22,48
RAYCREEK	14	18,43
REVIVAL	D1	10,79
Rhone	15	44
Richell Valeria	46	63
RIVER TAW	21	23,47
Rix Harrier	28	52

Rix Hawk	26	51	Teesdale H	25	51
Roelof Holwerda	65	76	The Dutch	65	76
ROVER T	33	33,54,55	Tora	29	52
SALLY	T1	9,10,11,14,77	Tower Conquest	40	59
Santuario	17	45	Trade Breeze	15	44
Sea Spray	37	56	Vechtborg	46	63
Seine	15	44	VIC 42	13	42
Sellin	34	54	WATER LILY	D2	10,79
SELLINA C	34	54	WHITONIA	41	28,59
Simba Vesta	17	45	WIB	28	52
Splash	46	63	WIGGS	31	26,54
SPRINGFINCH	18	45	WILKS	25	26,50,51
Studland	12	42	WIRIS	35	26,56
Subro Vesta	17	45	WIS	26	50,51
Swanage	10	41	X	10	41
Taillefer	13	42	X 73	12	42
Tanja Holwerda	65	76	YARVIC	13	15,18,42,43

Hoocrest (2) at Rochester. *[Author]*